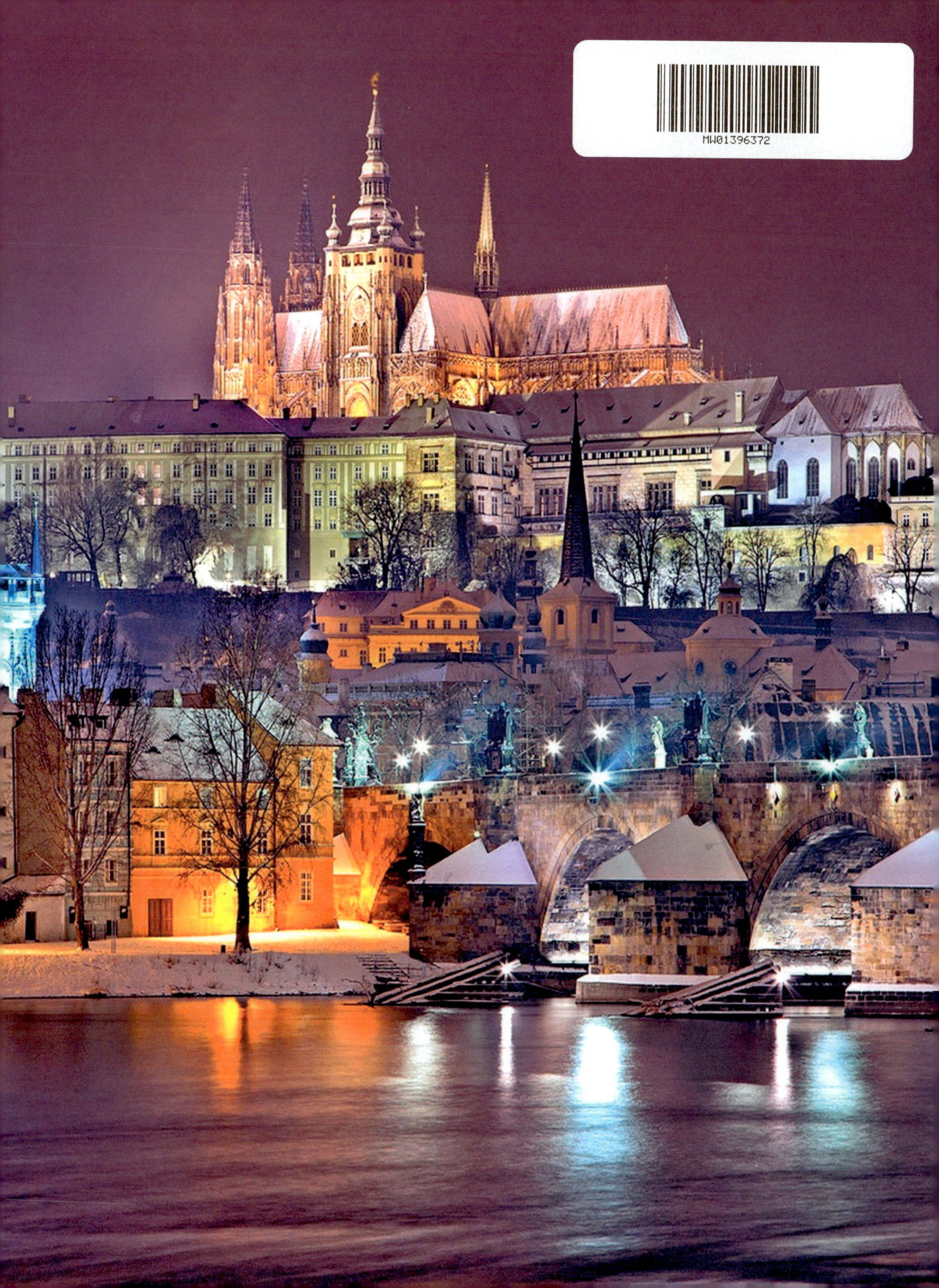

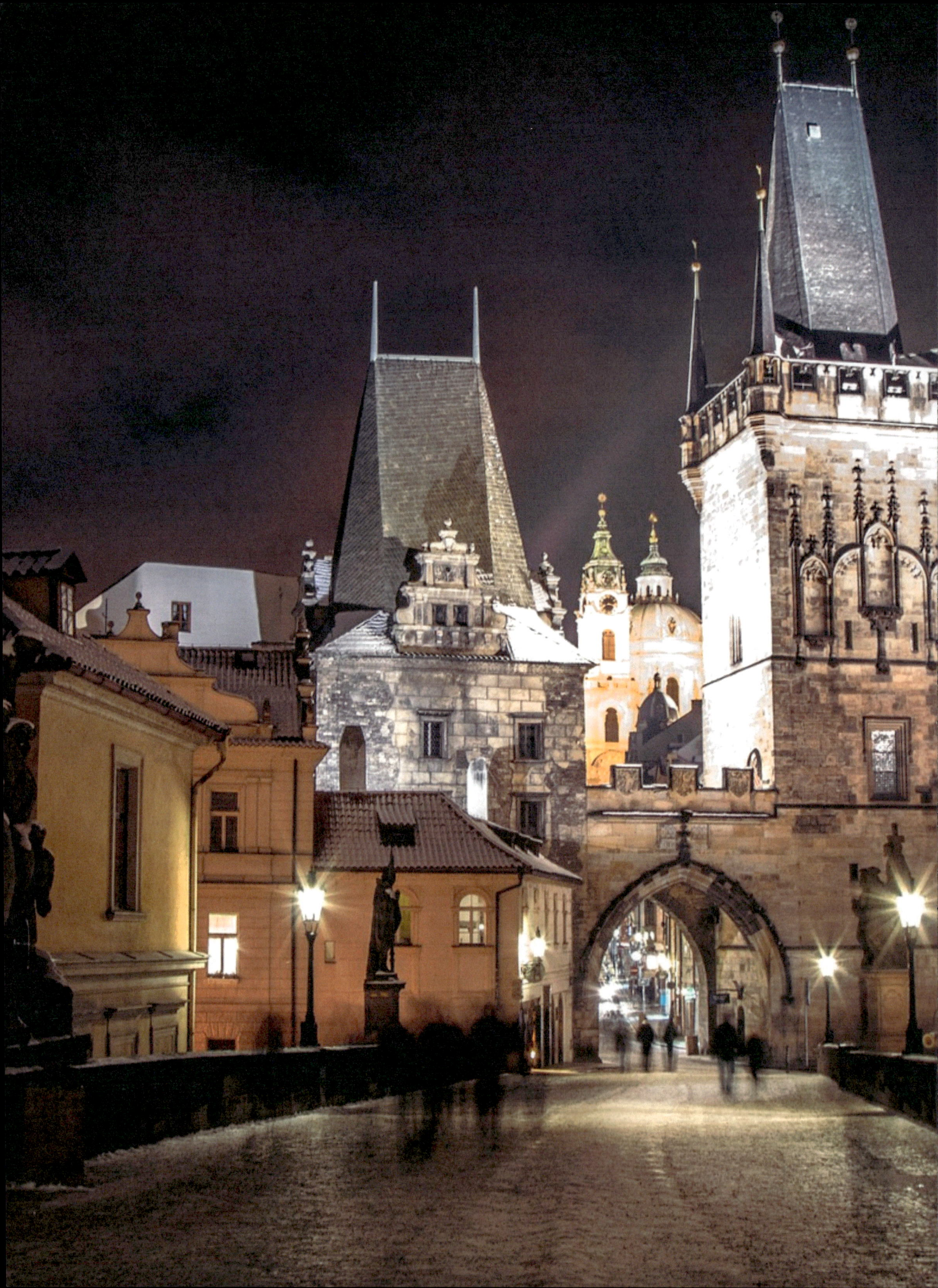

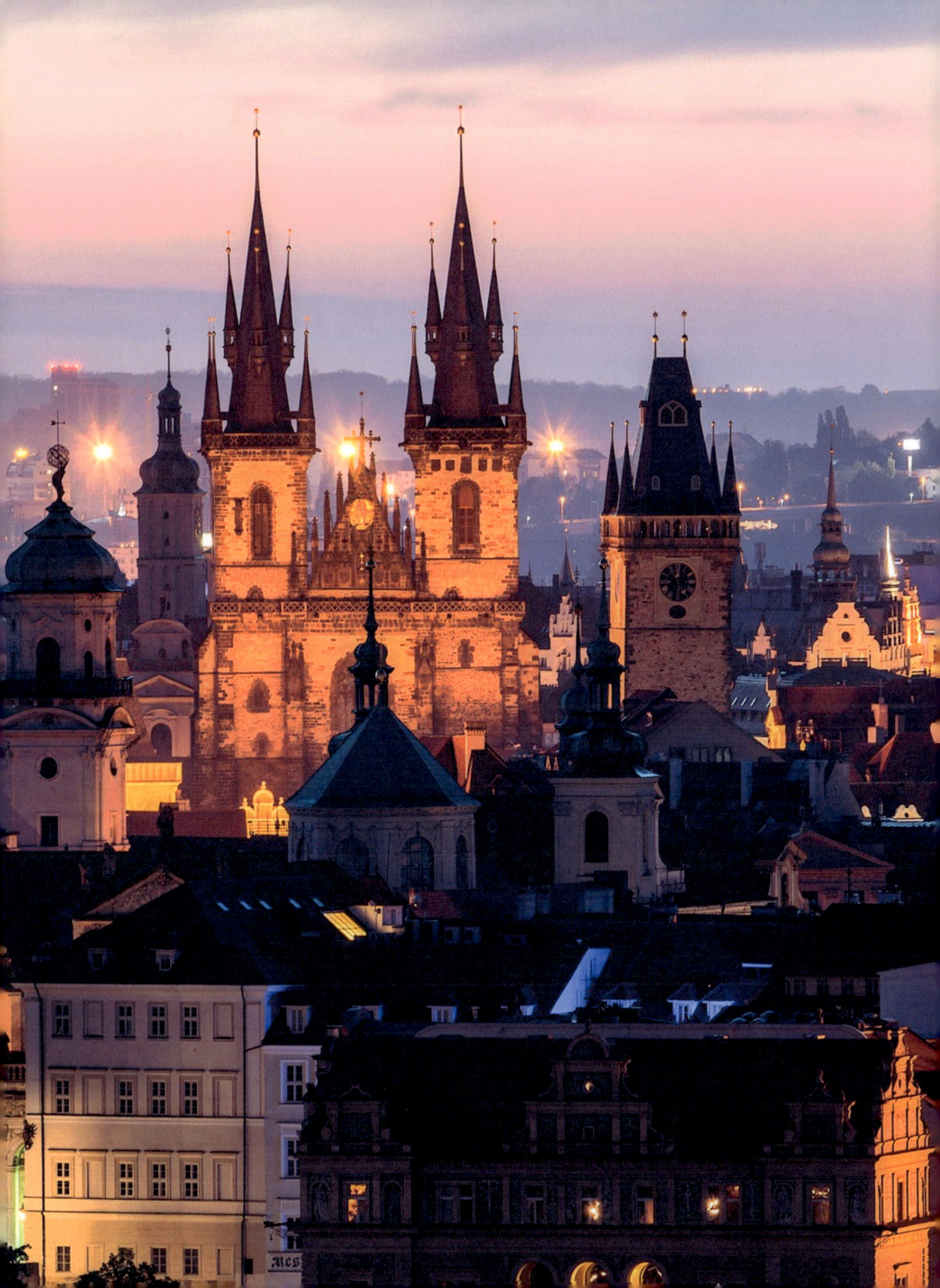

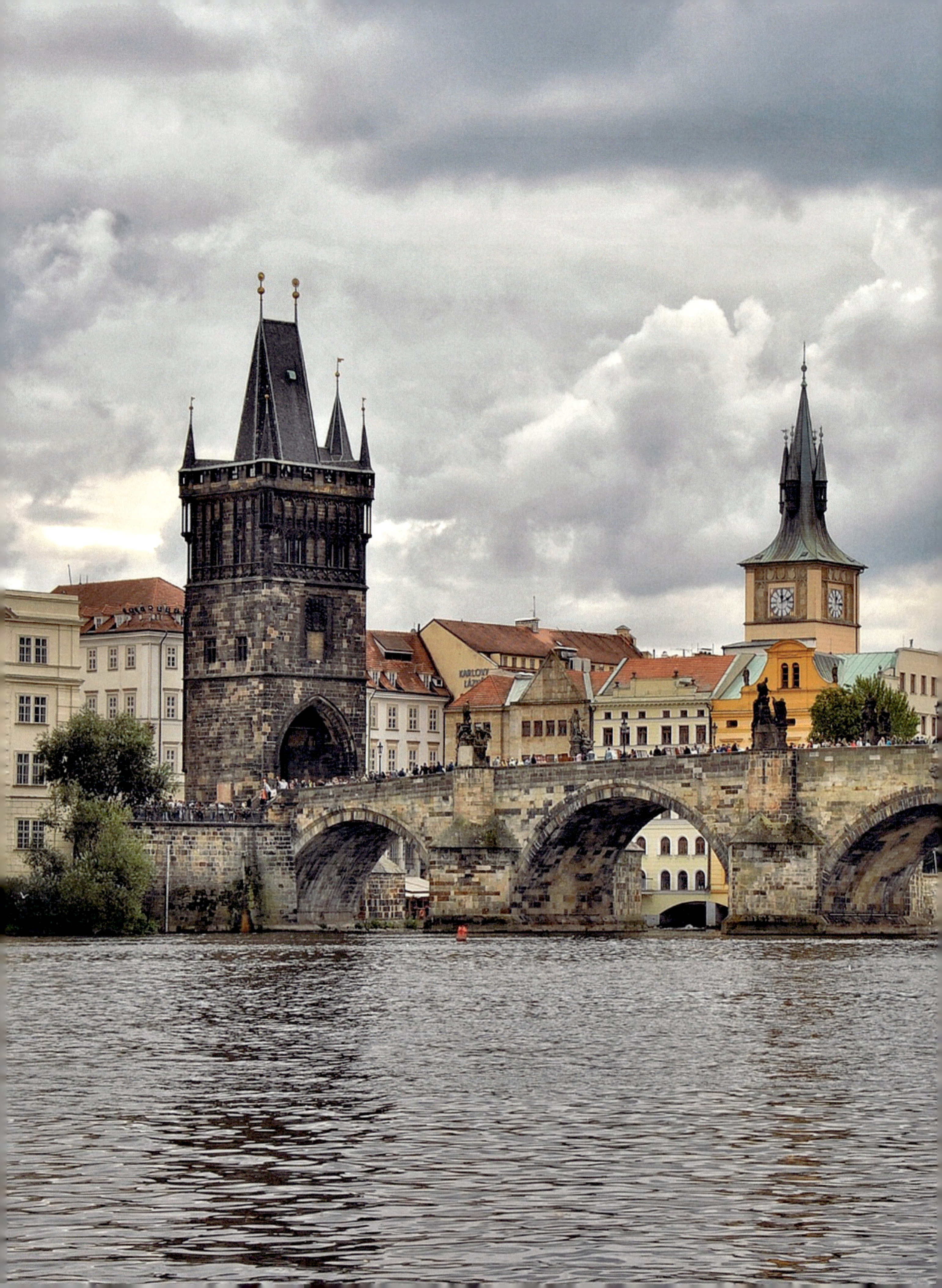

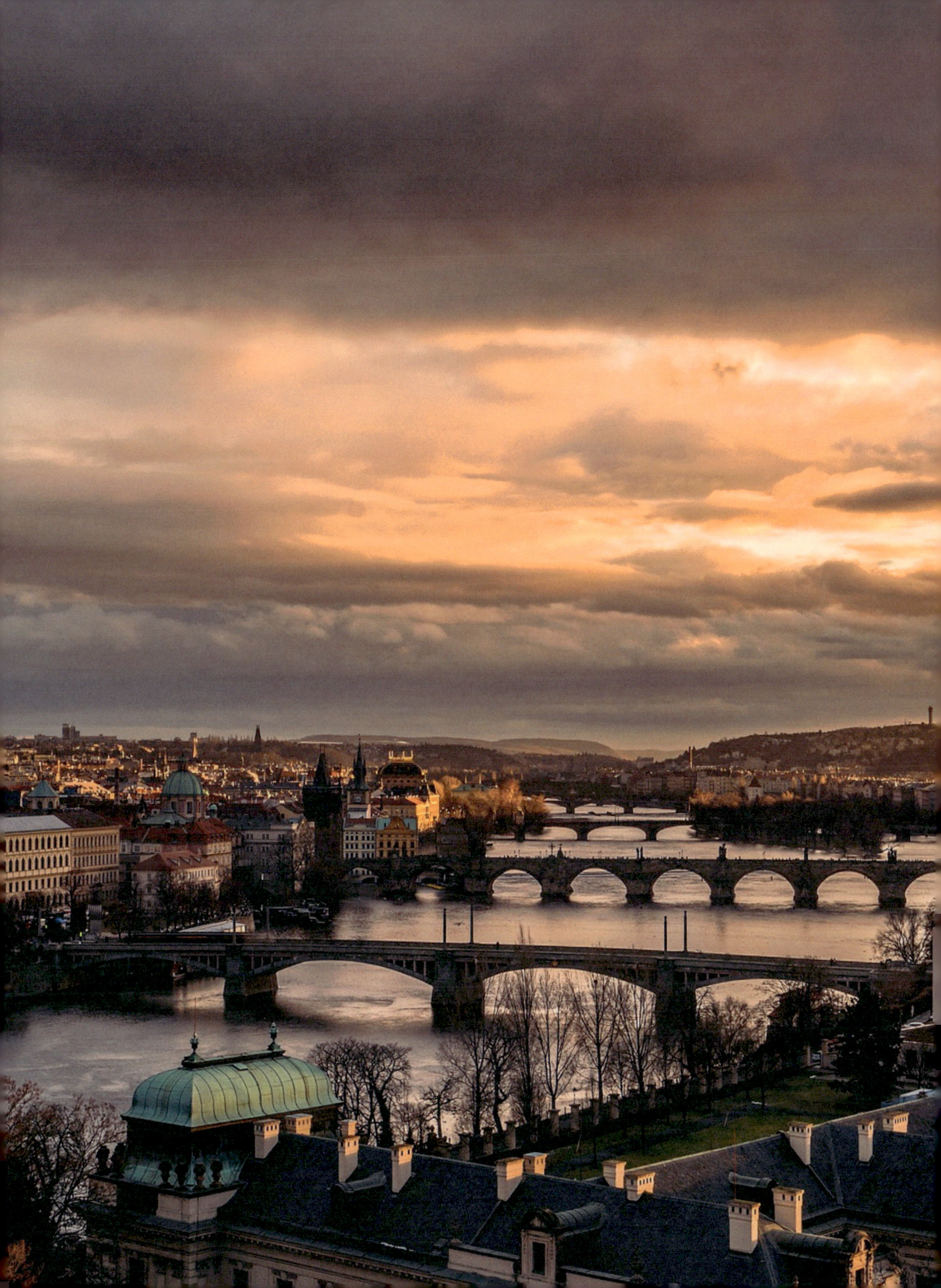

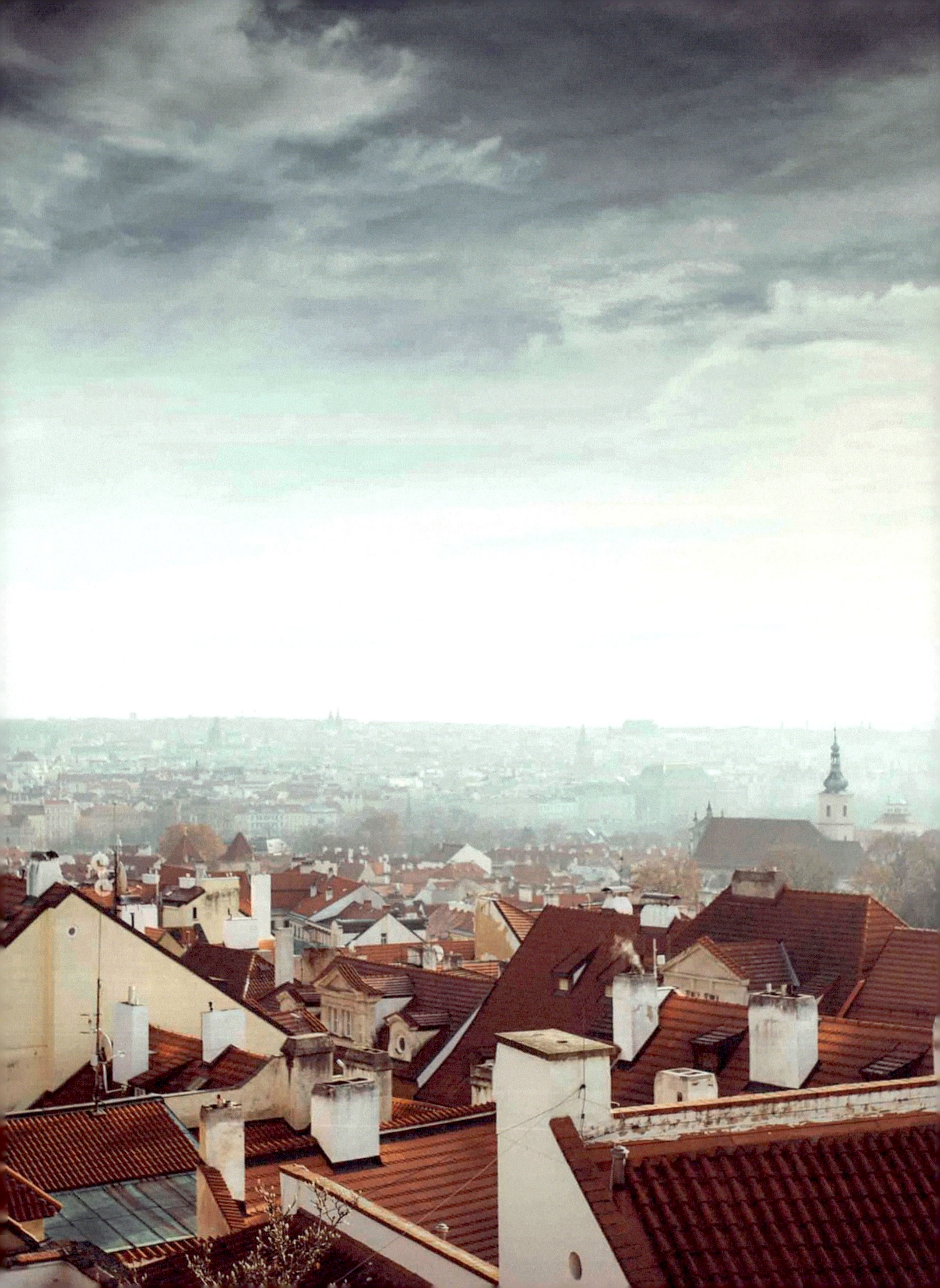

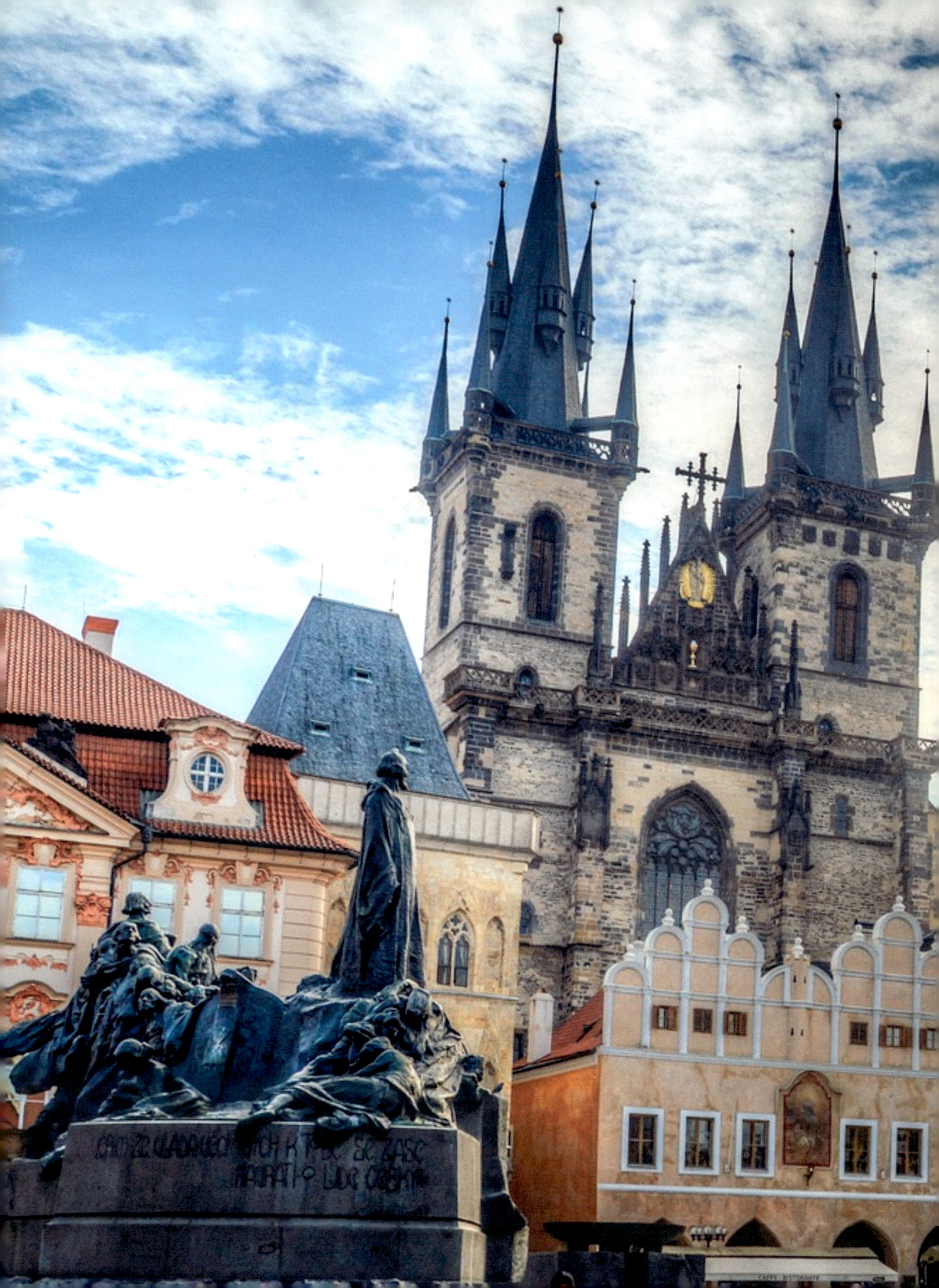

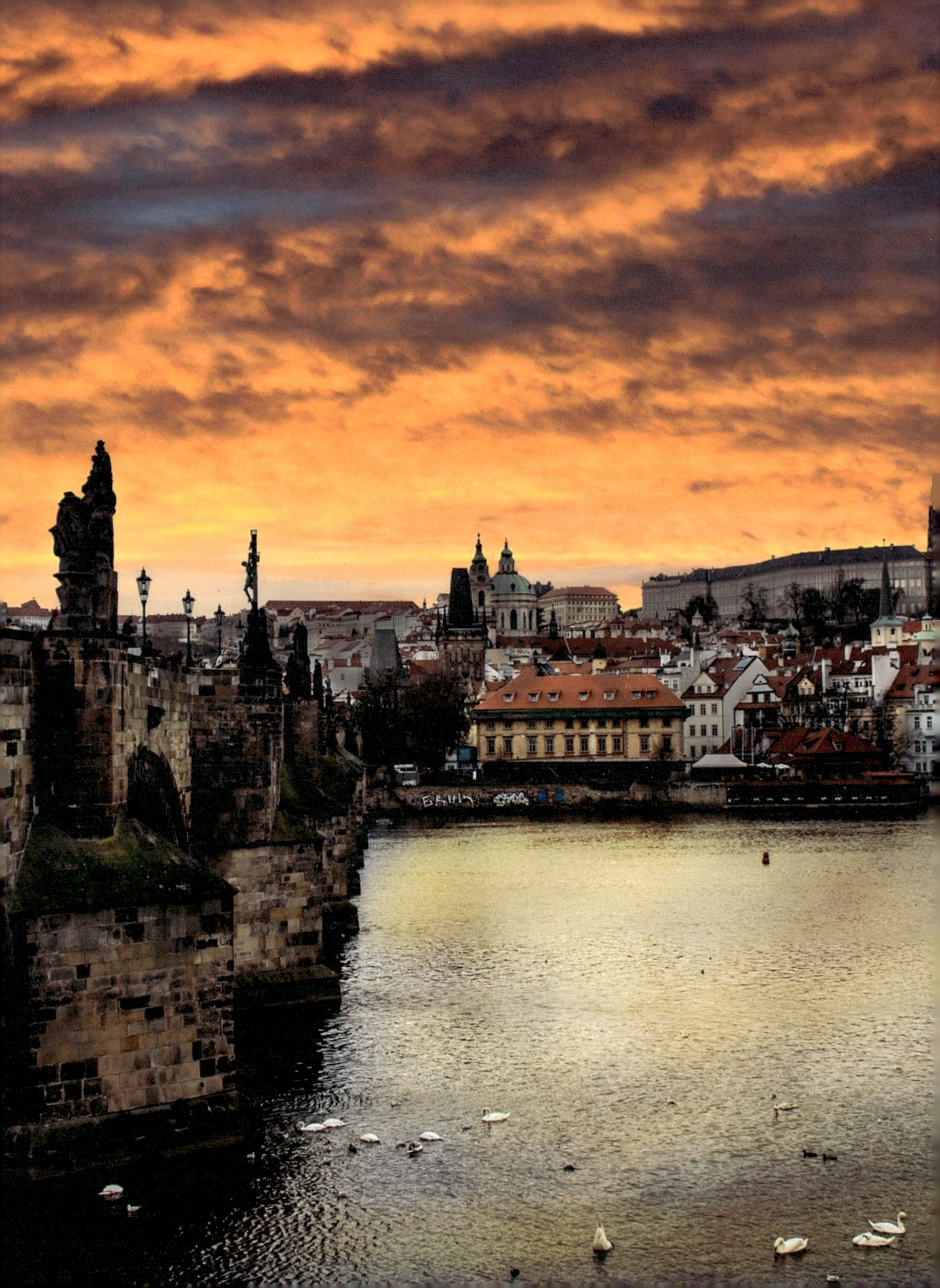

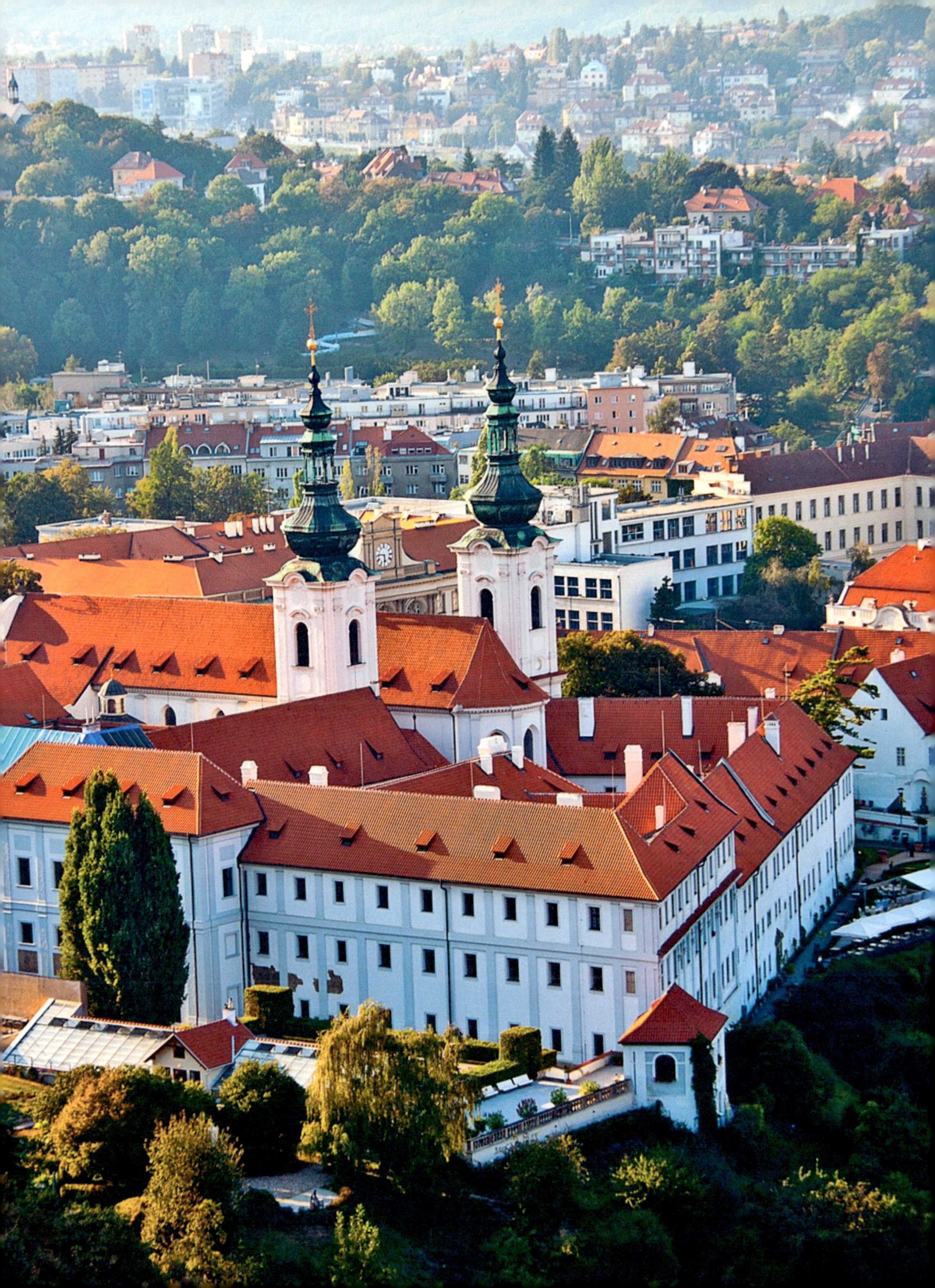

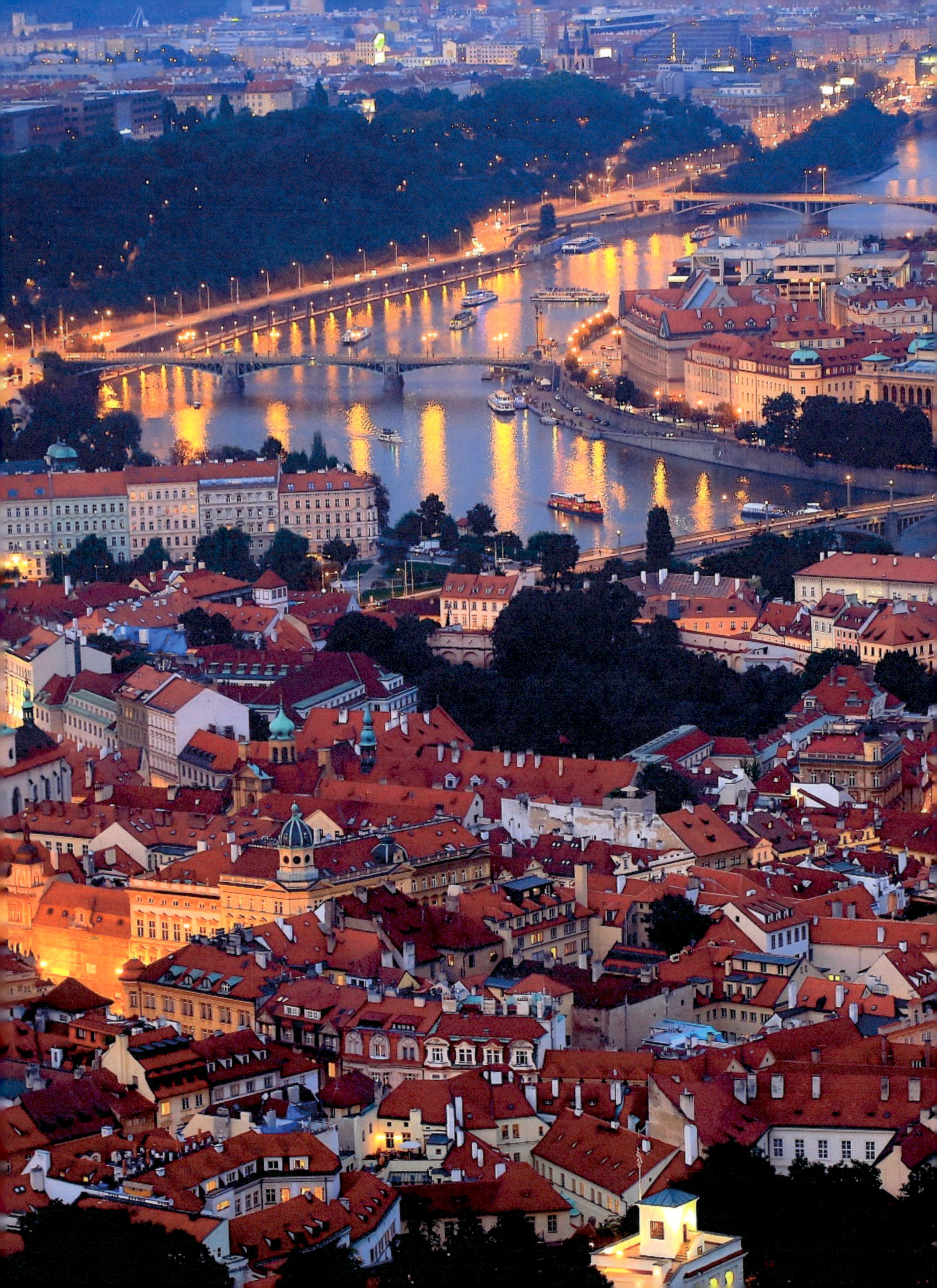

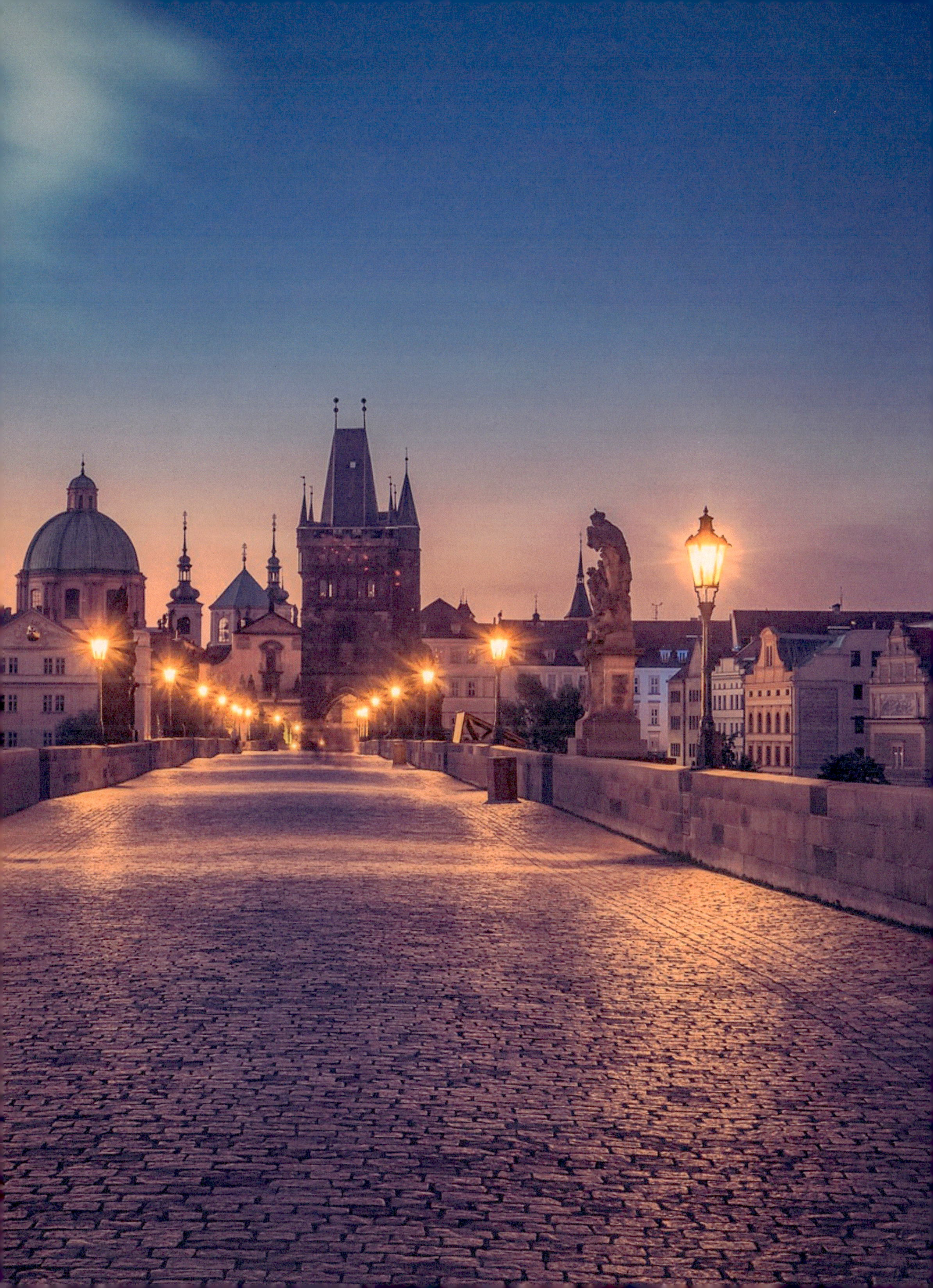

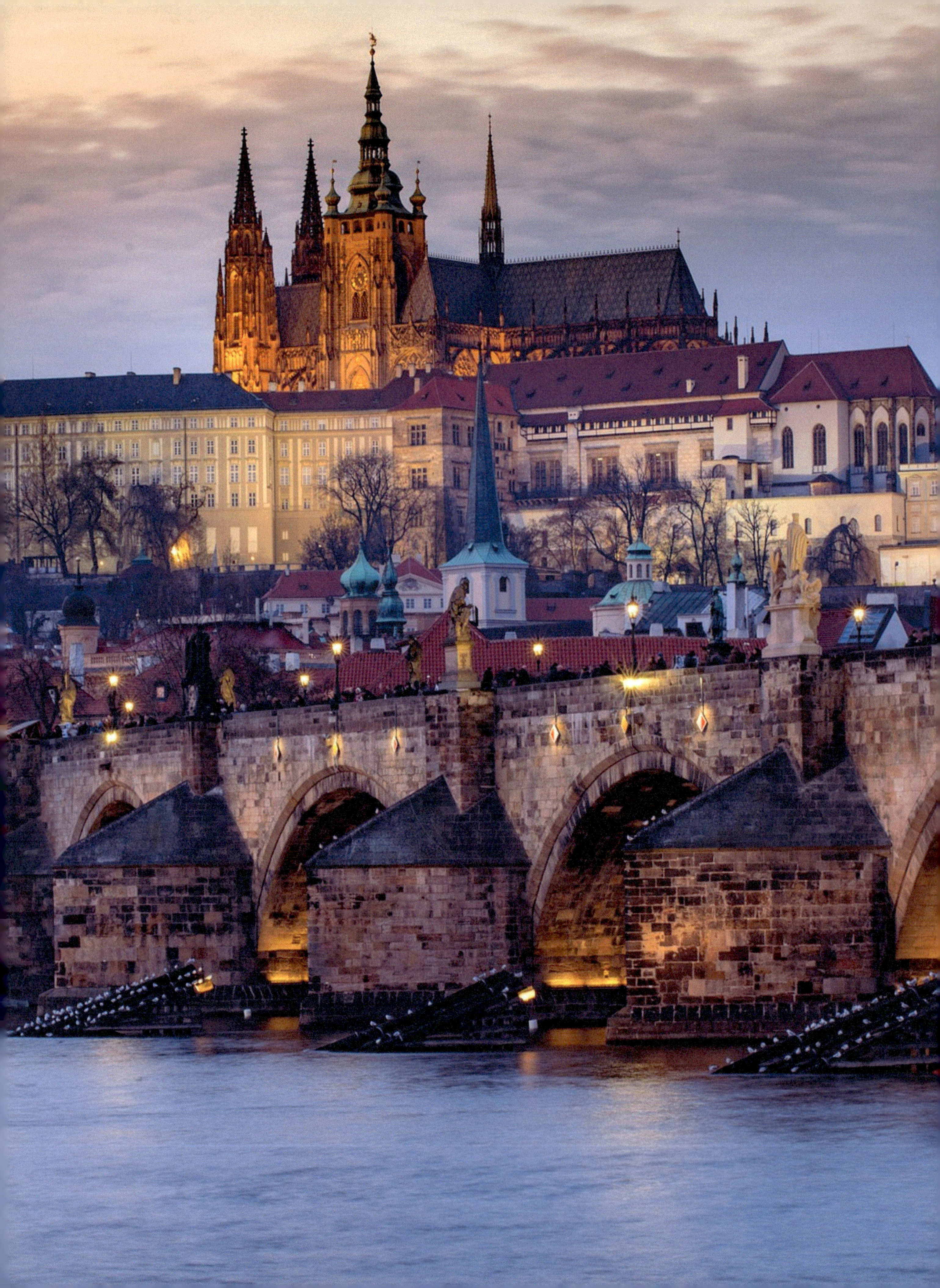

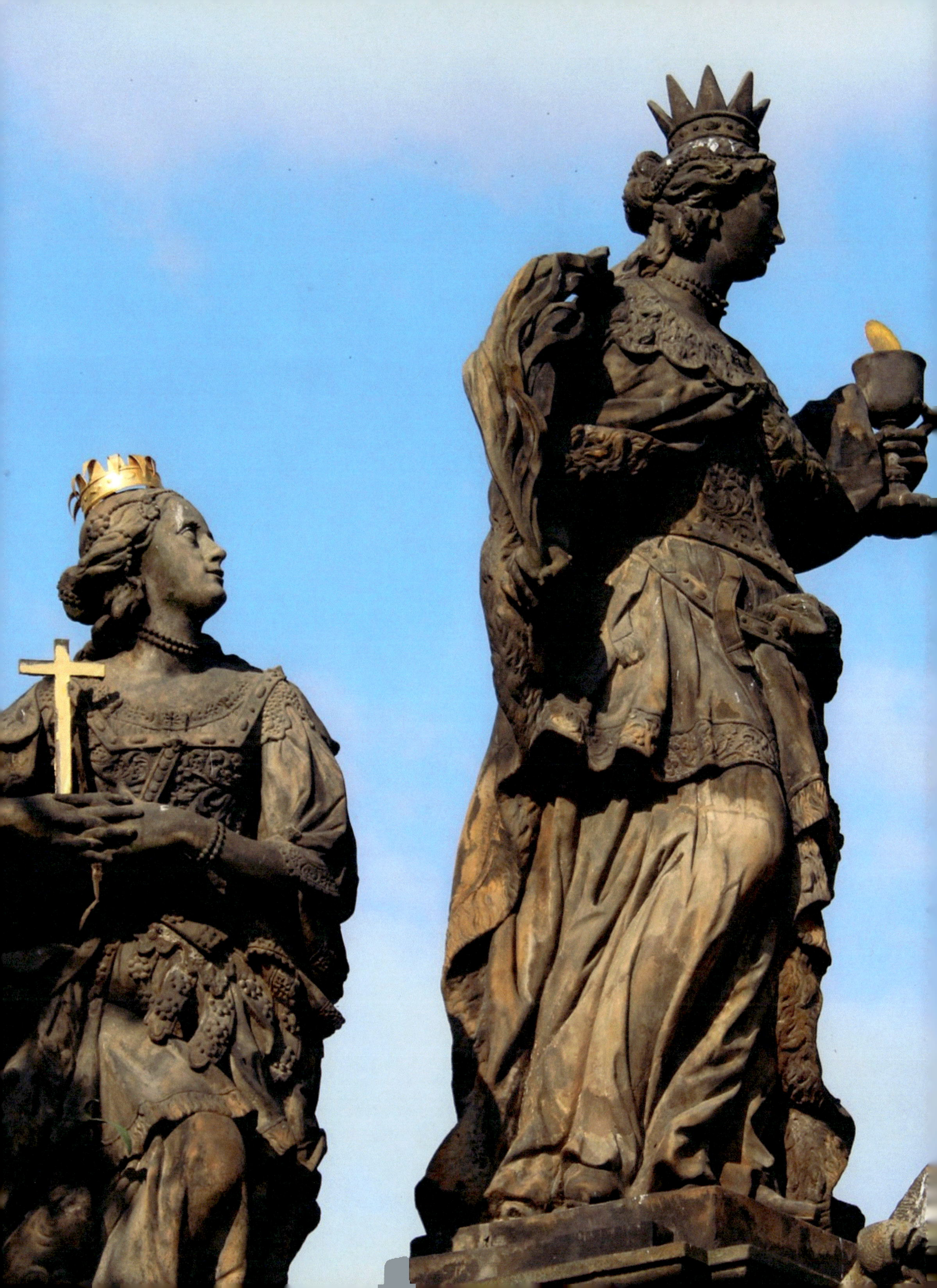

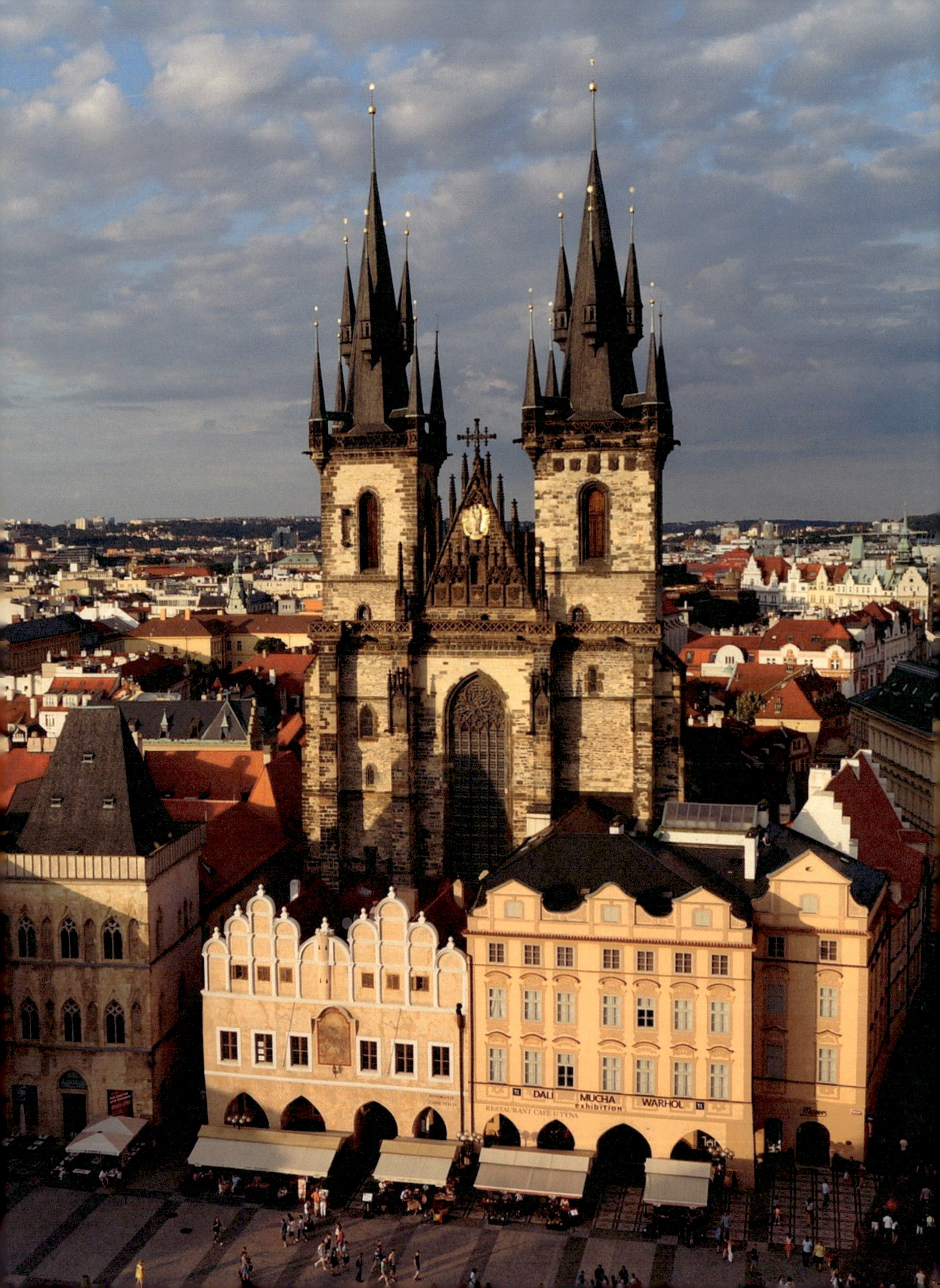
DALI
MUCHA
exhibition
WARHOL

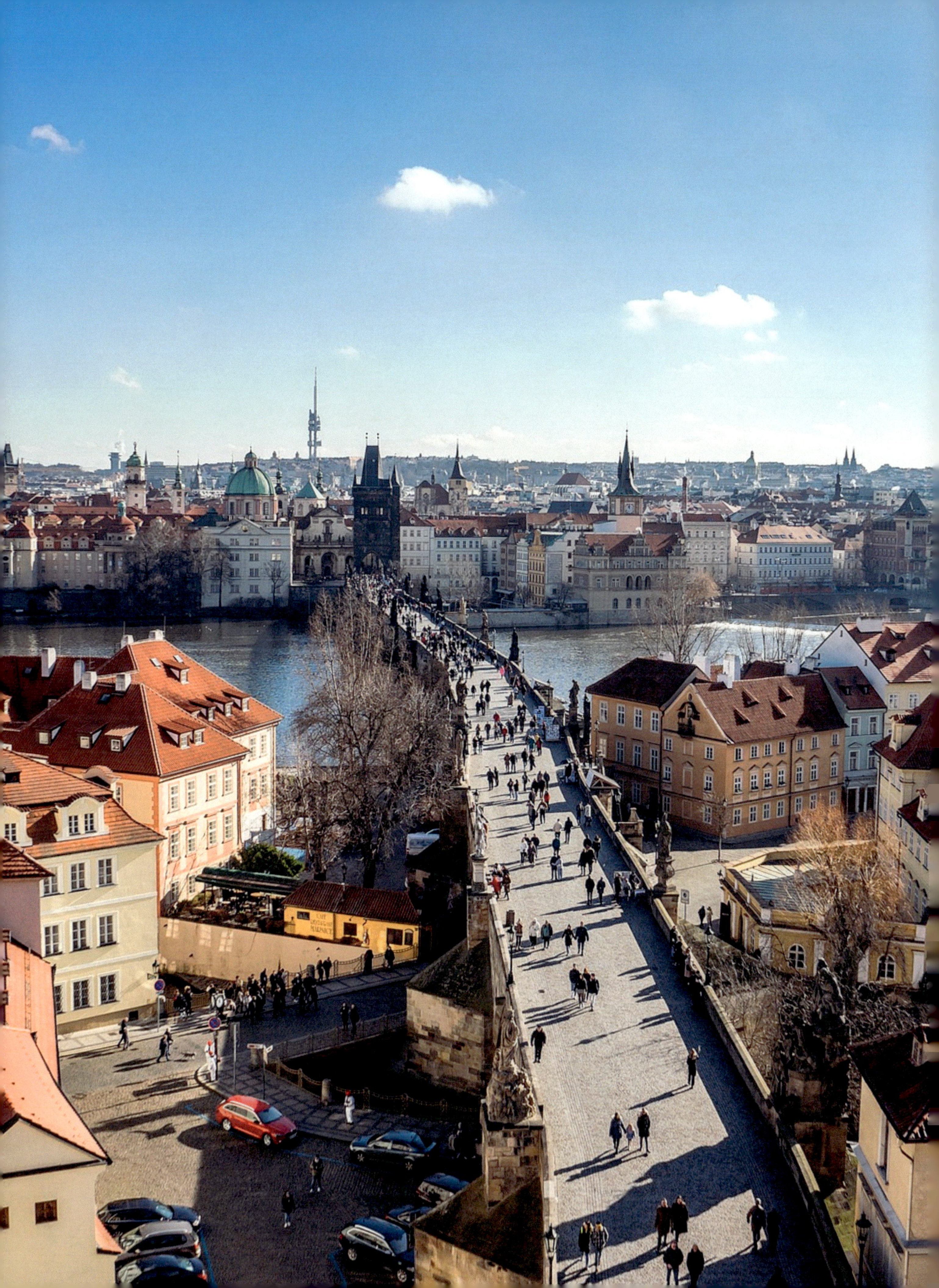

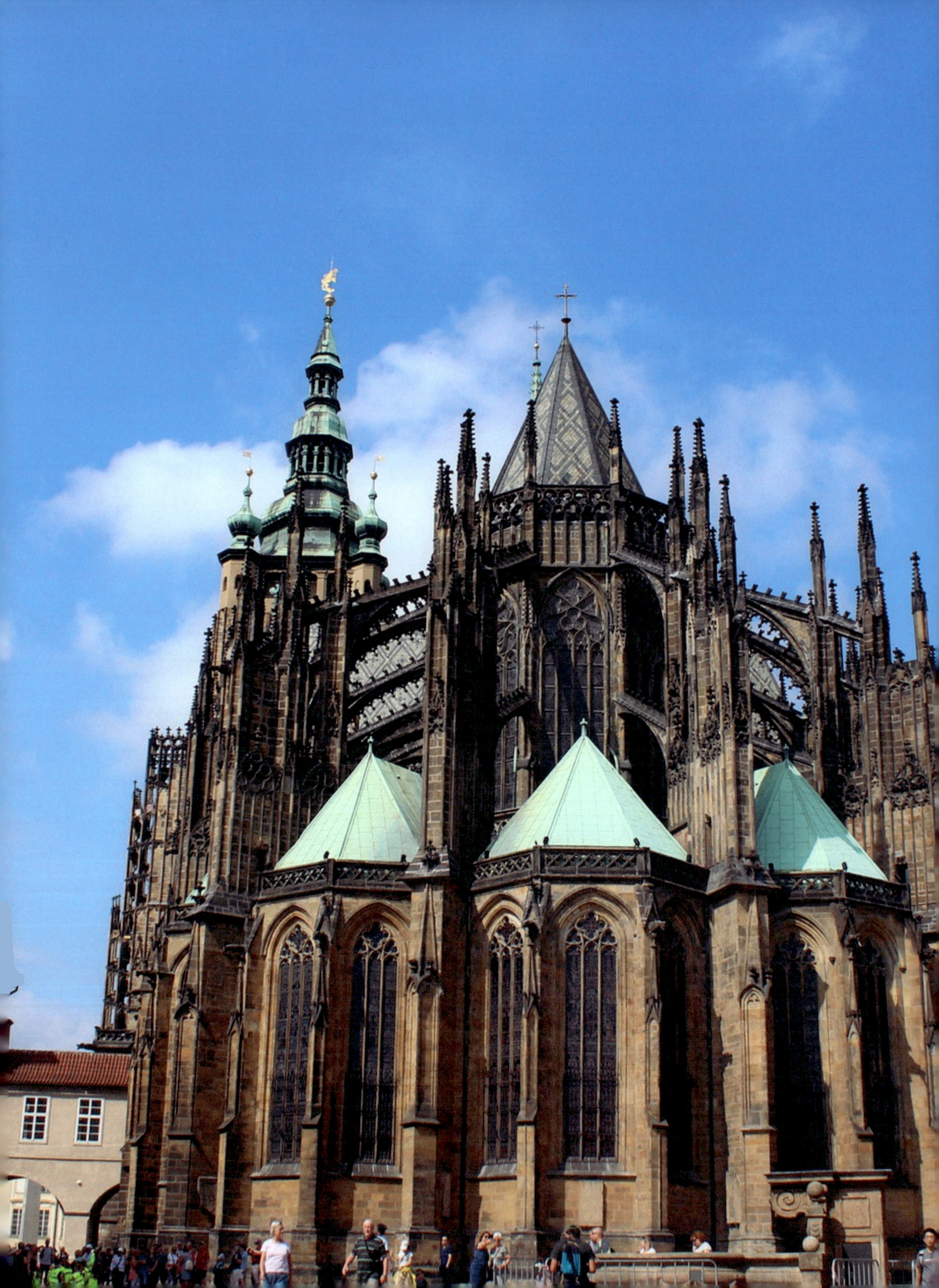

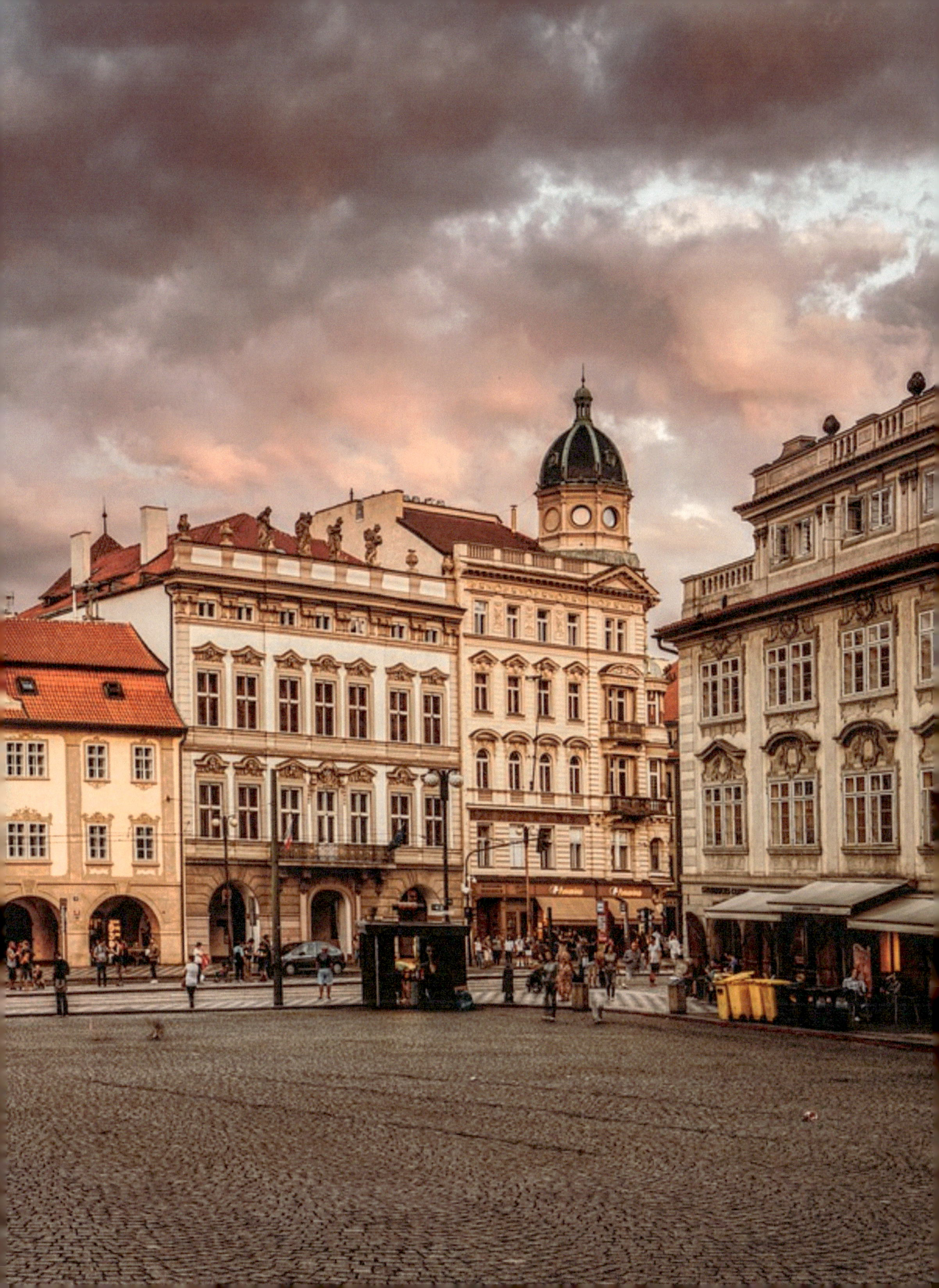

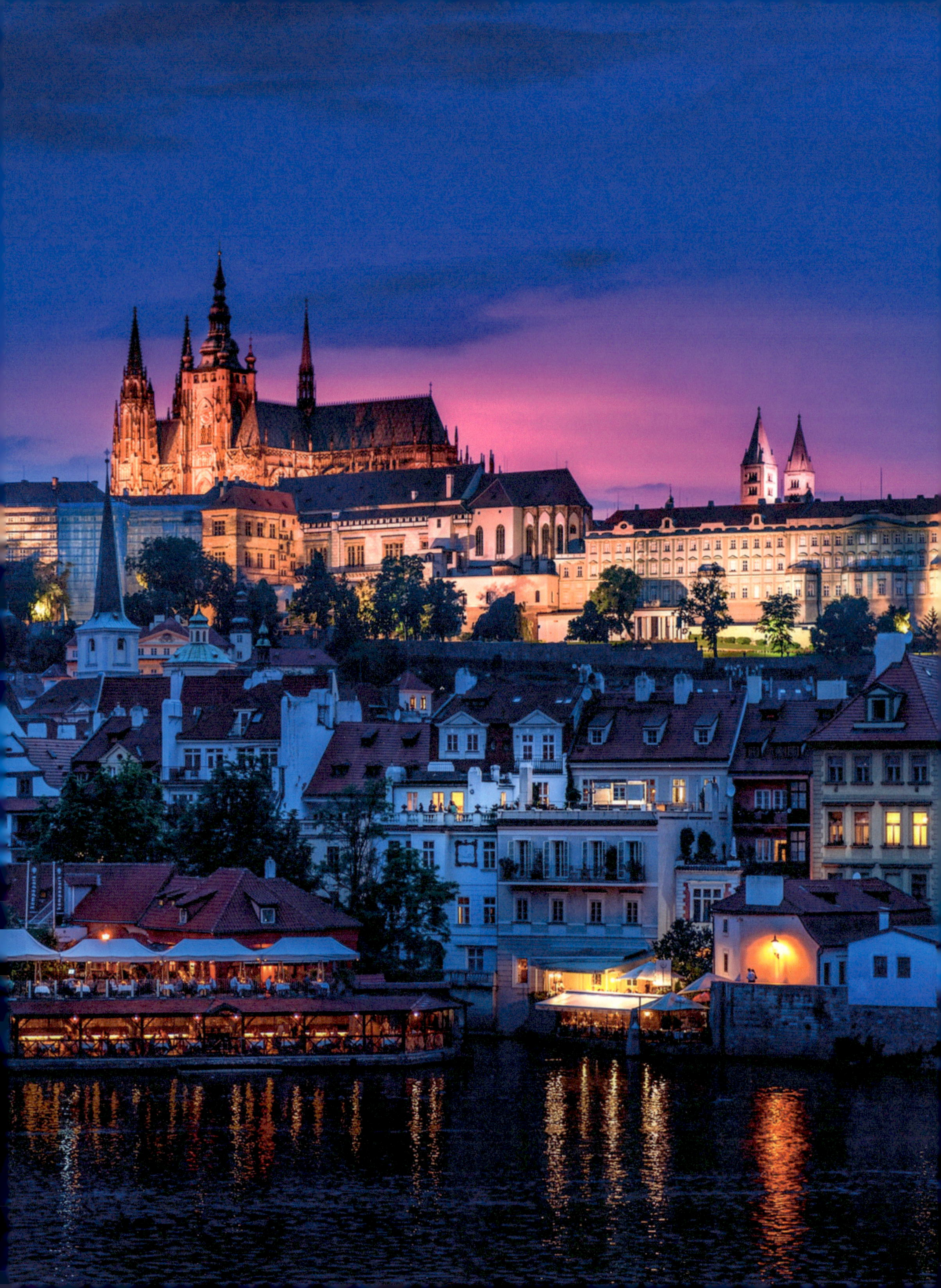

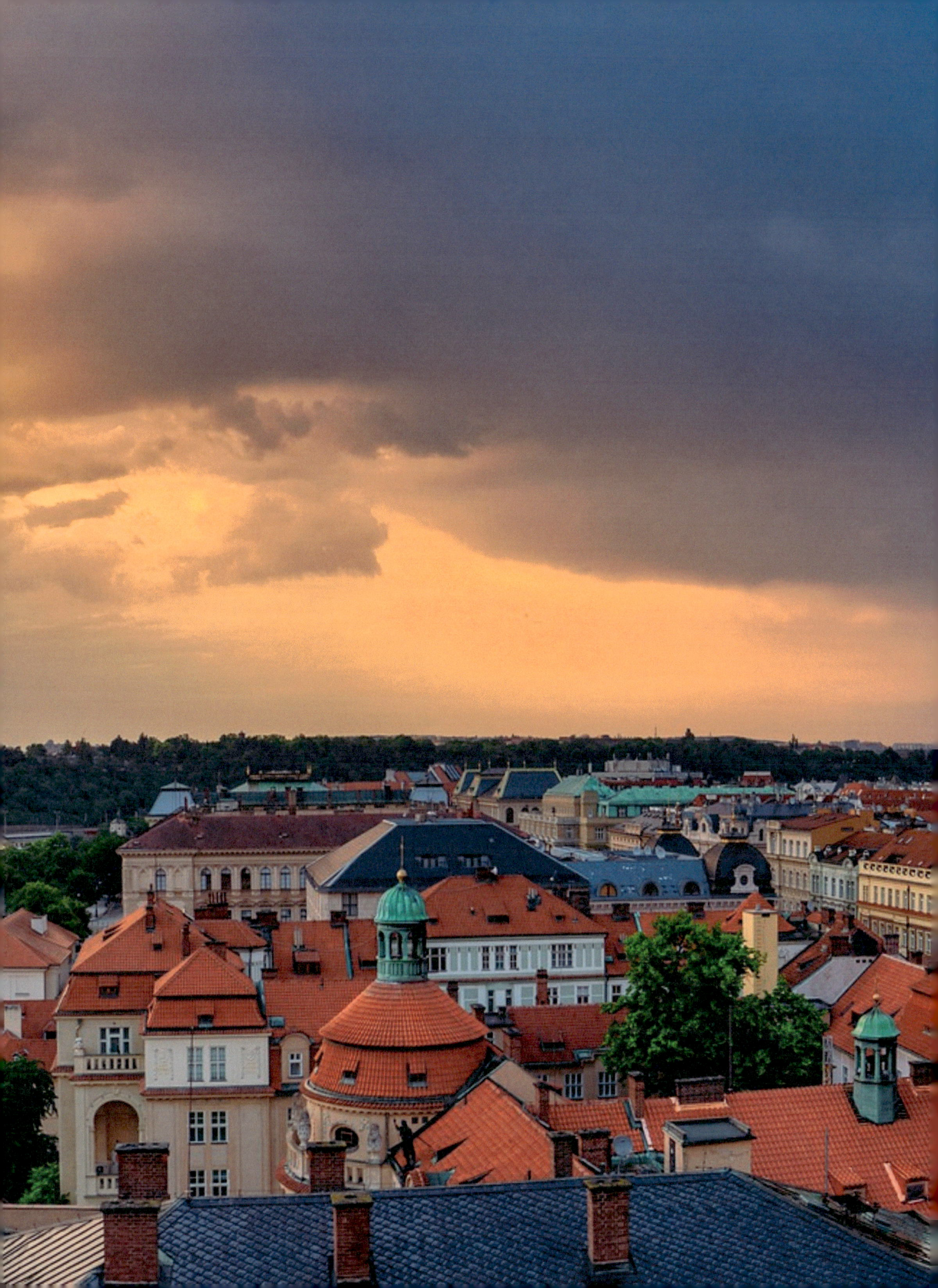

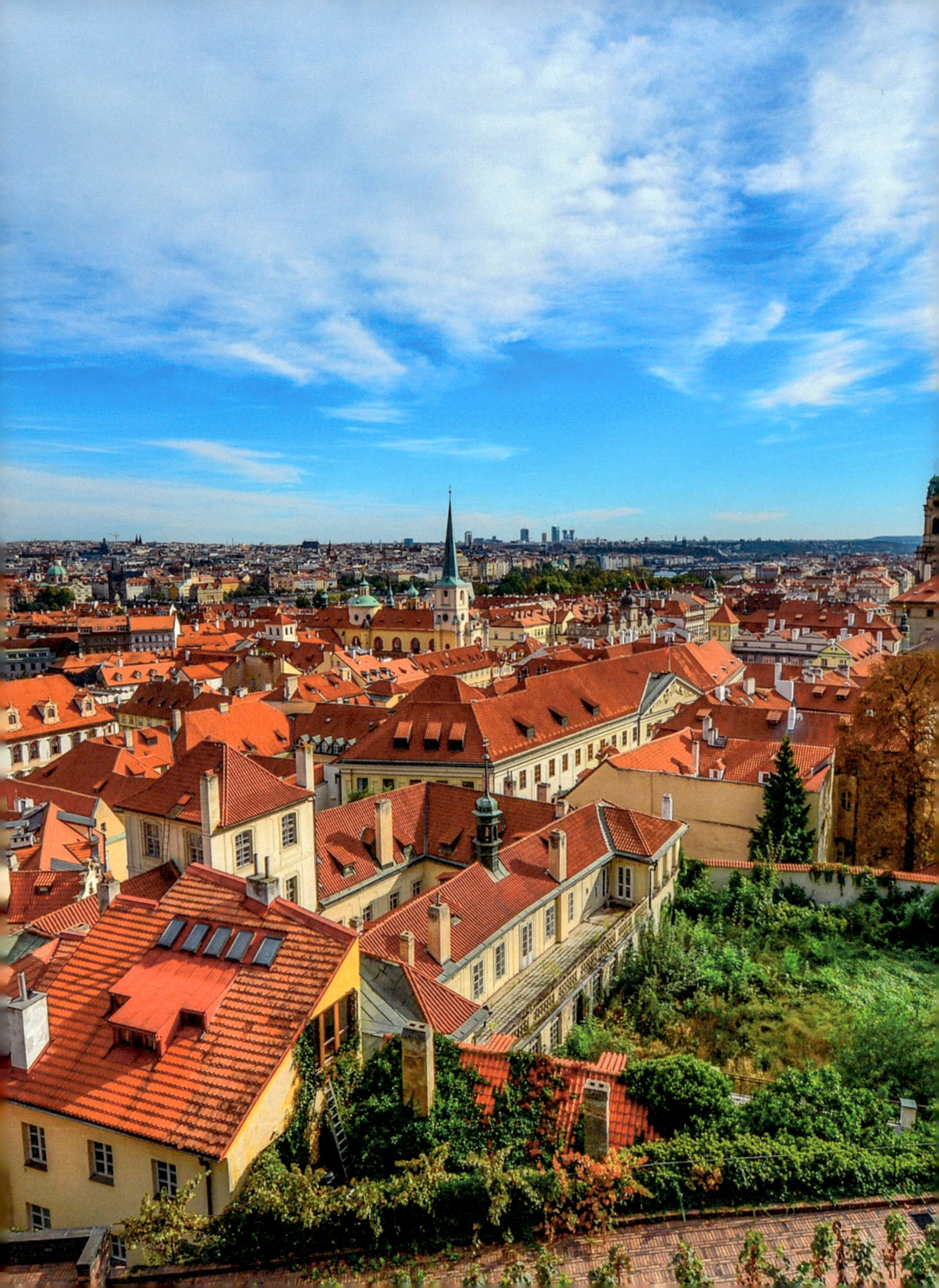

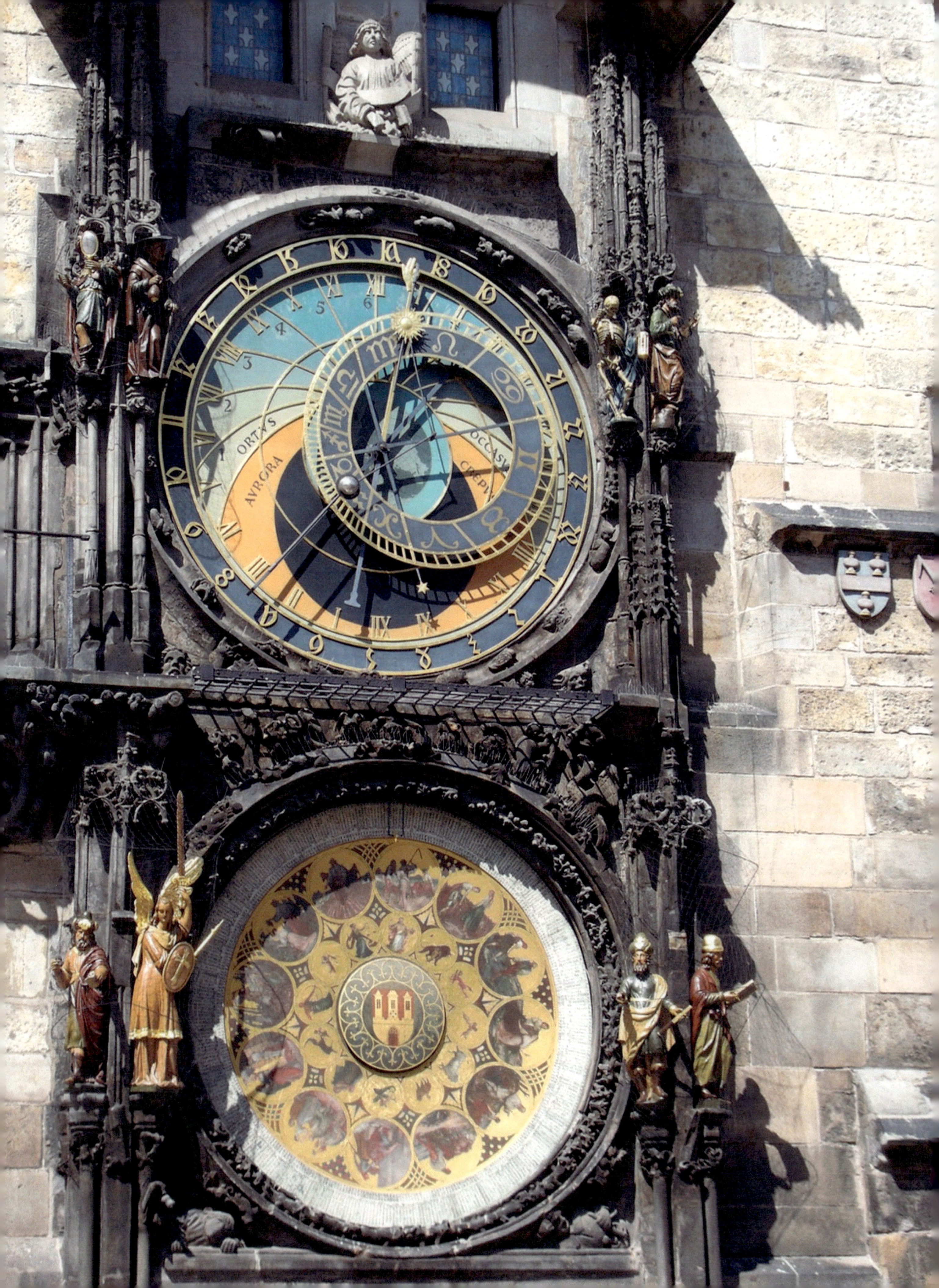
ORTVS
AVRORA

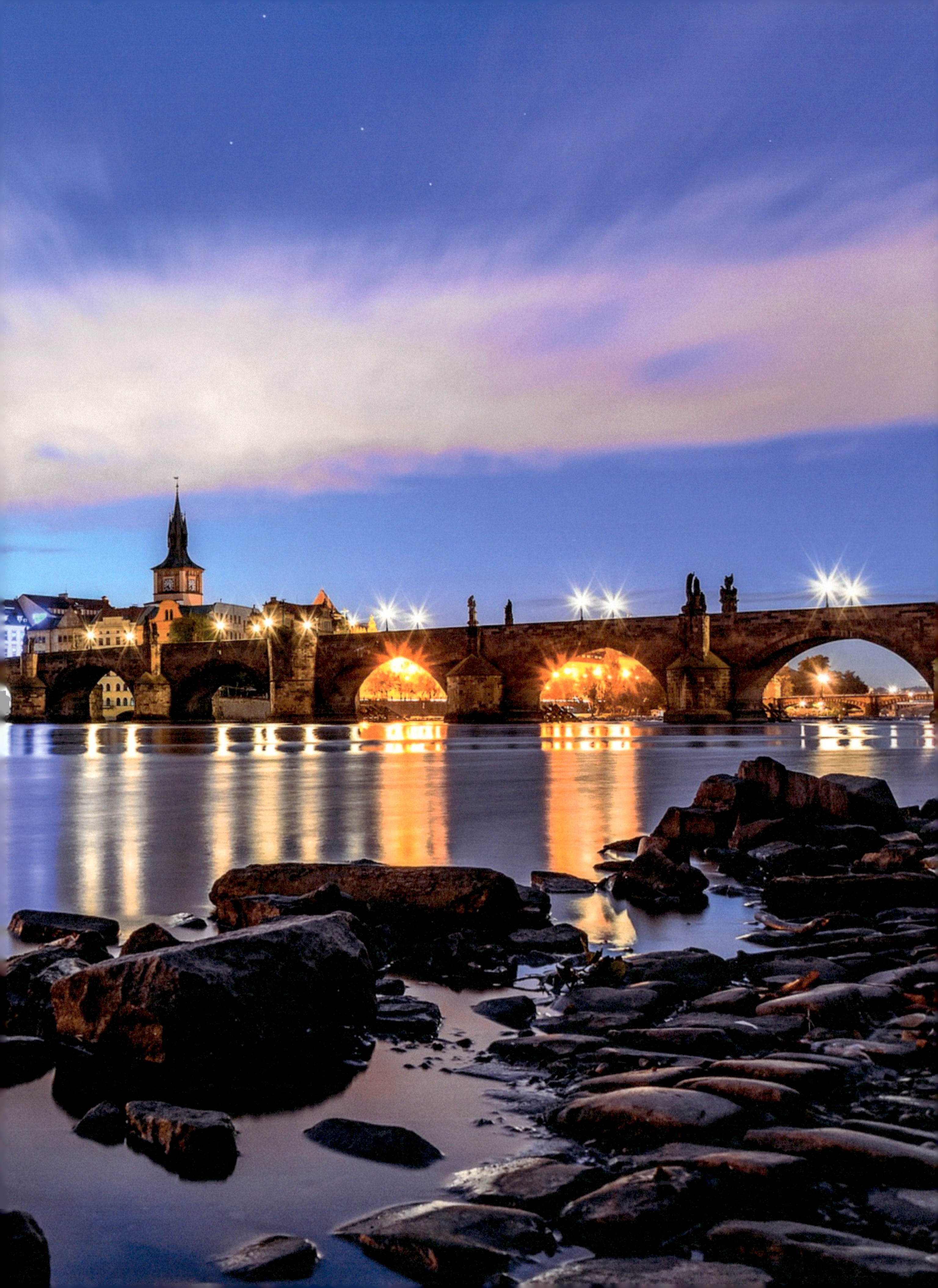

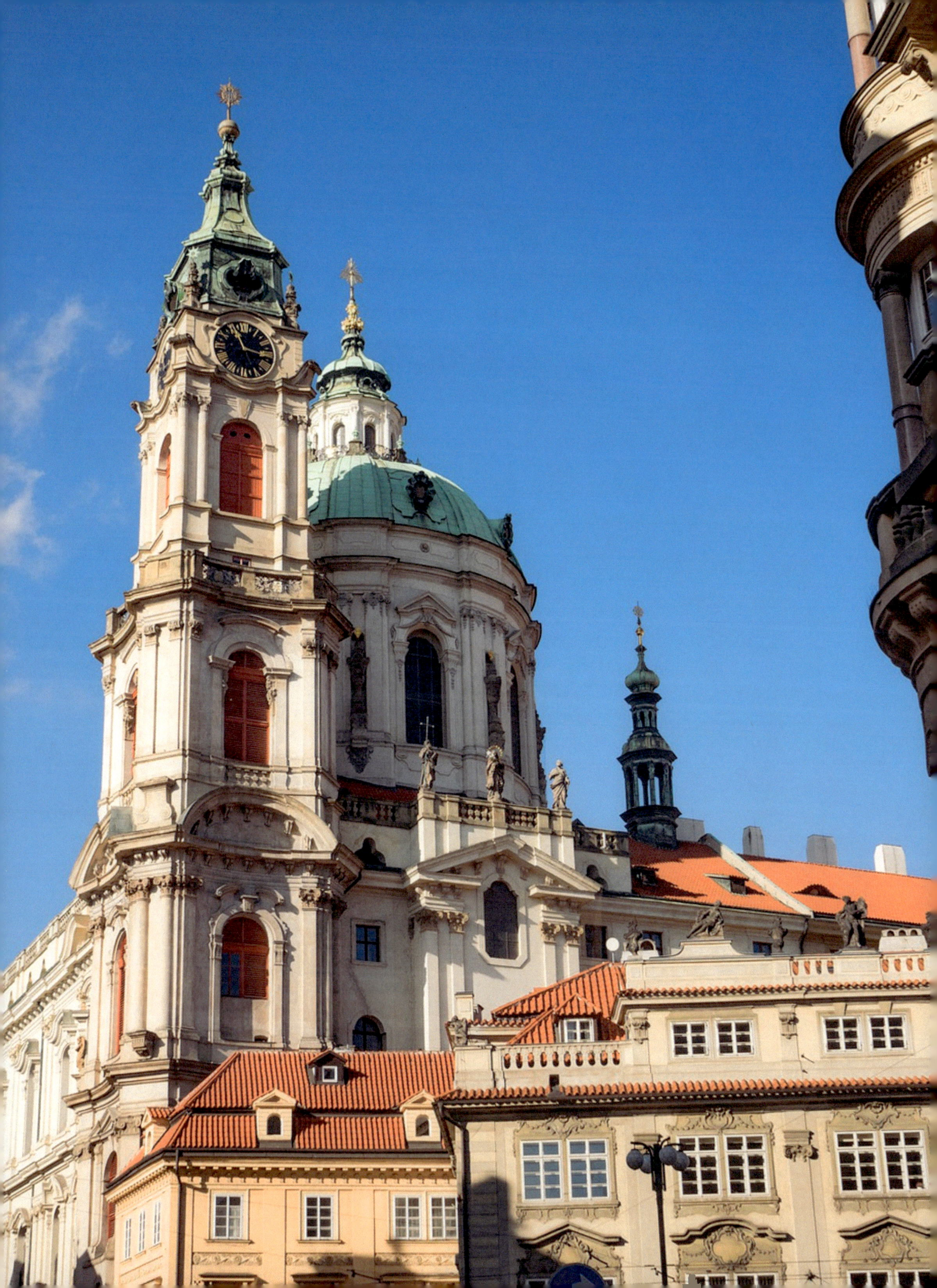

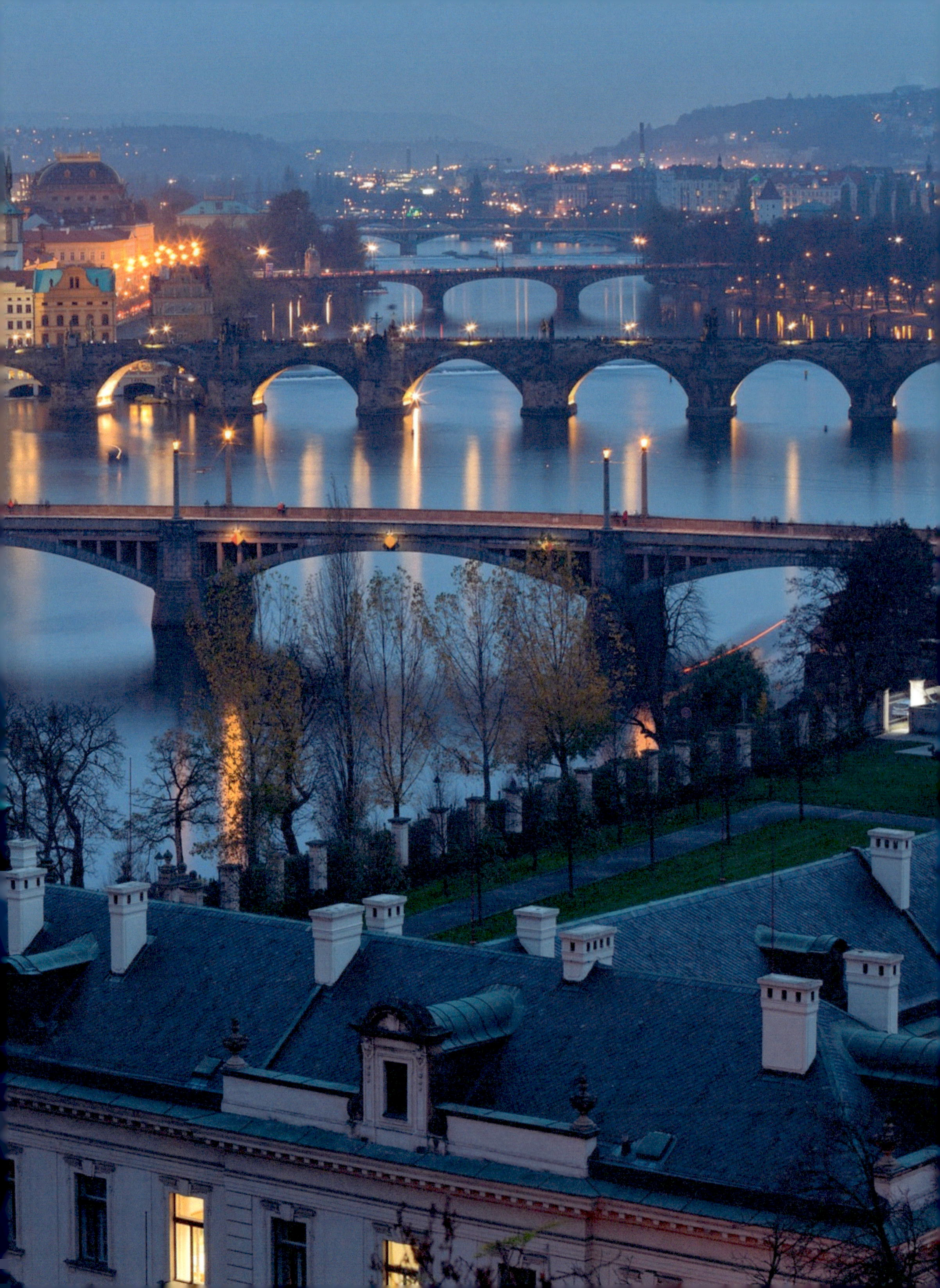

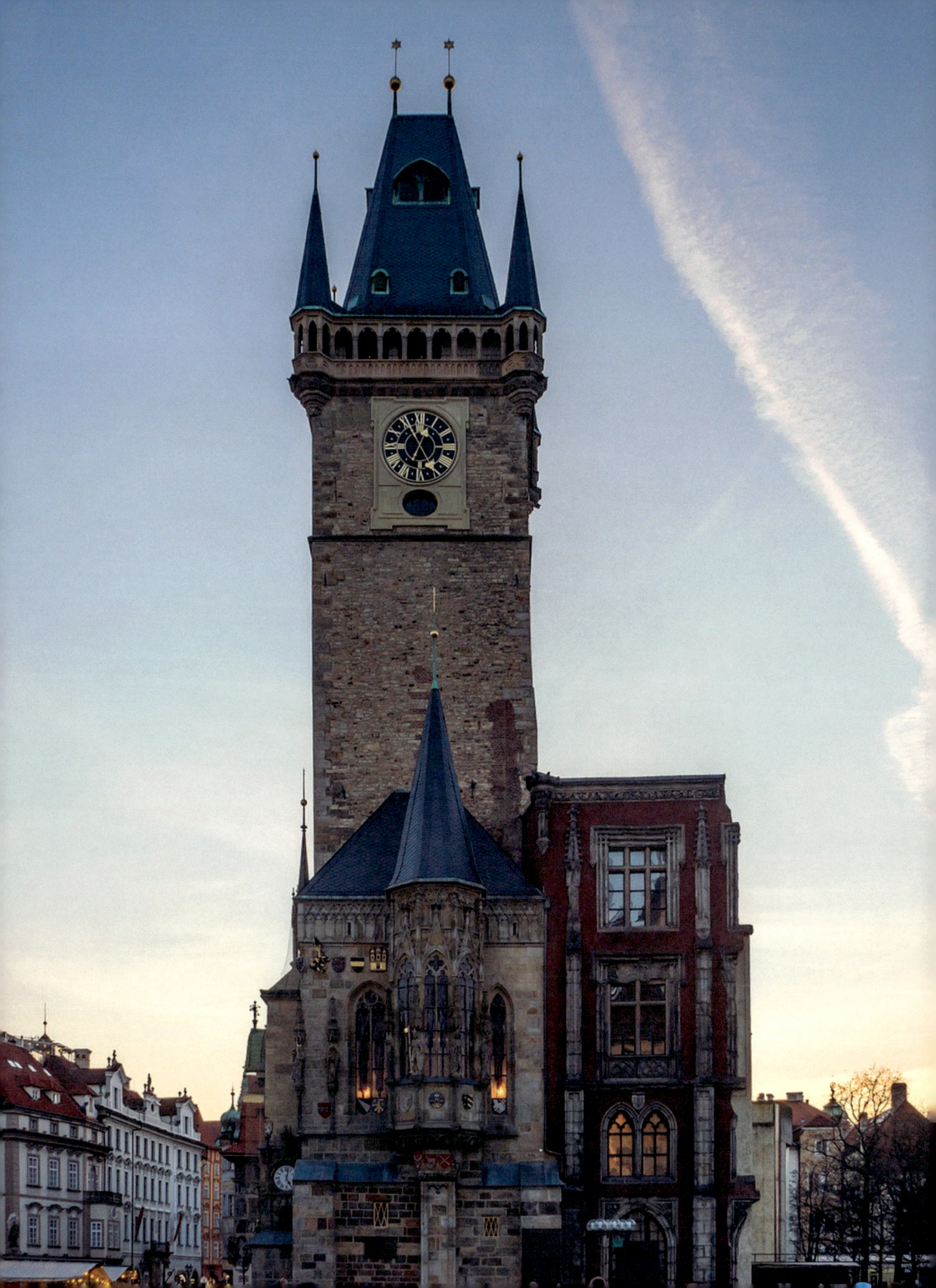

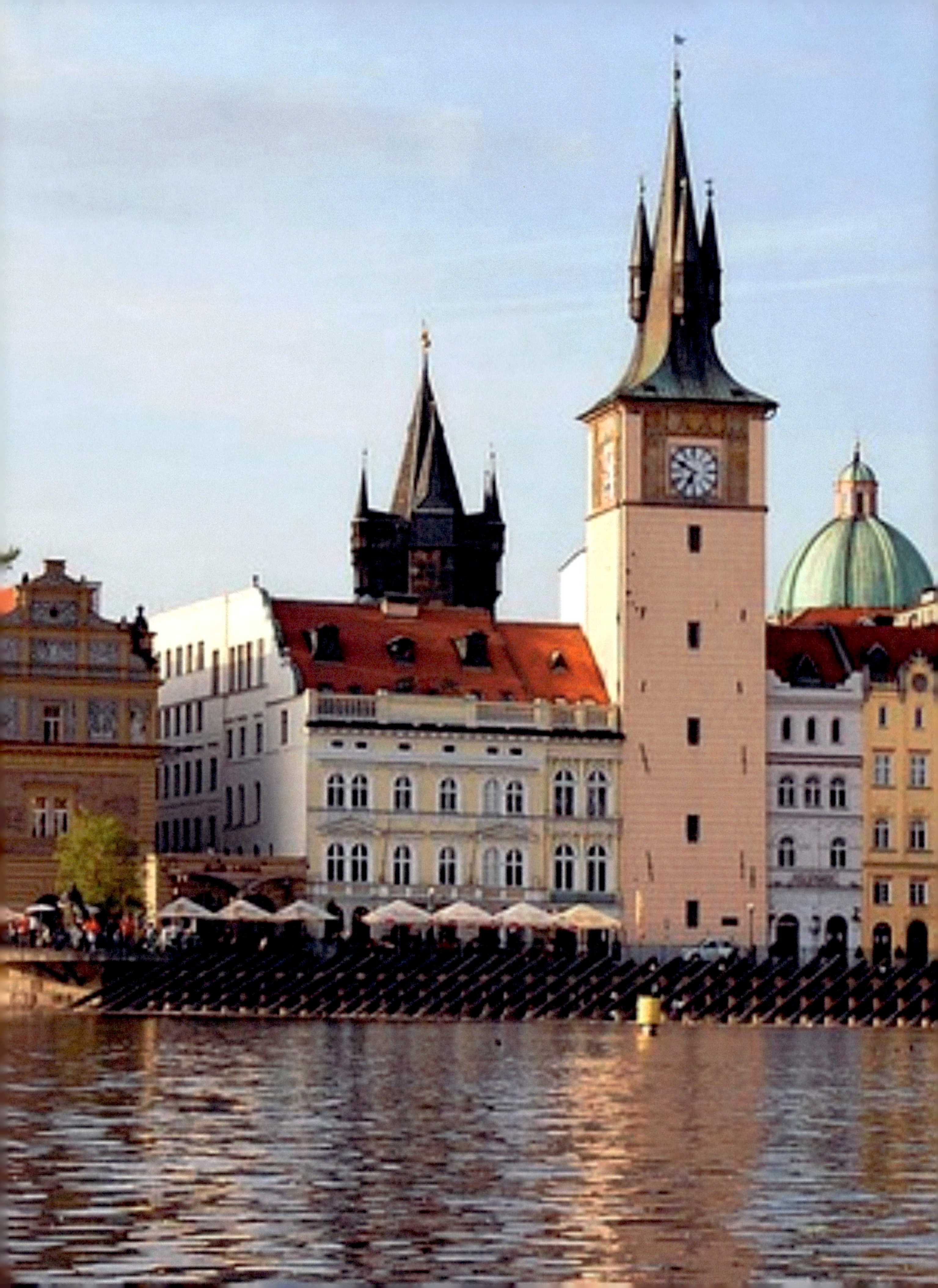

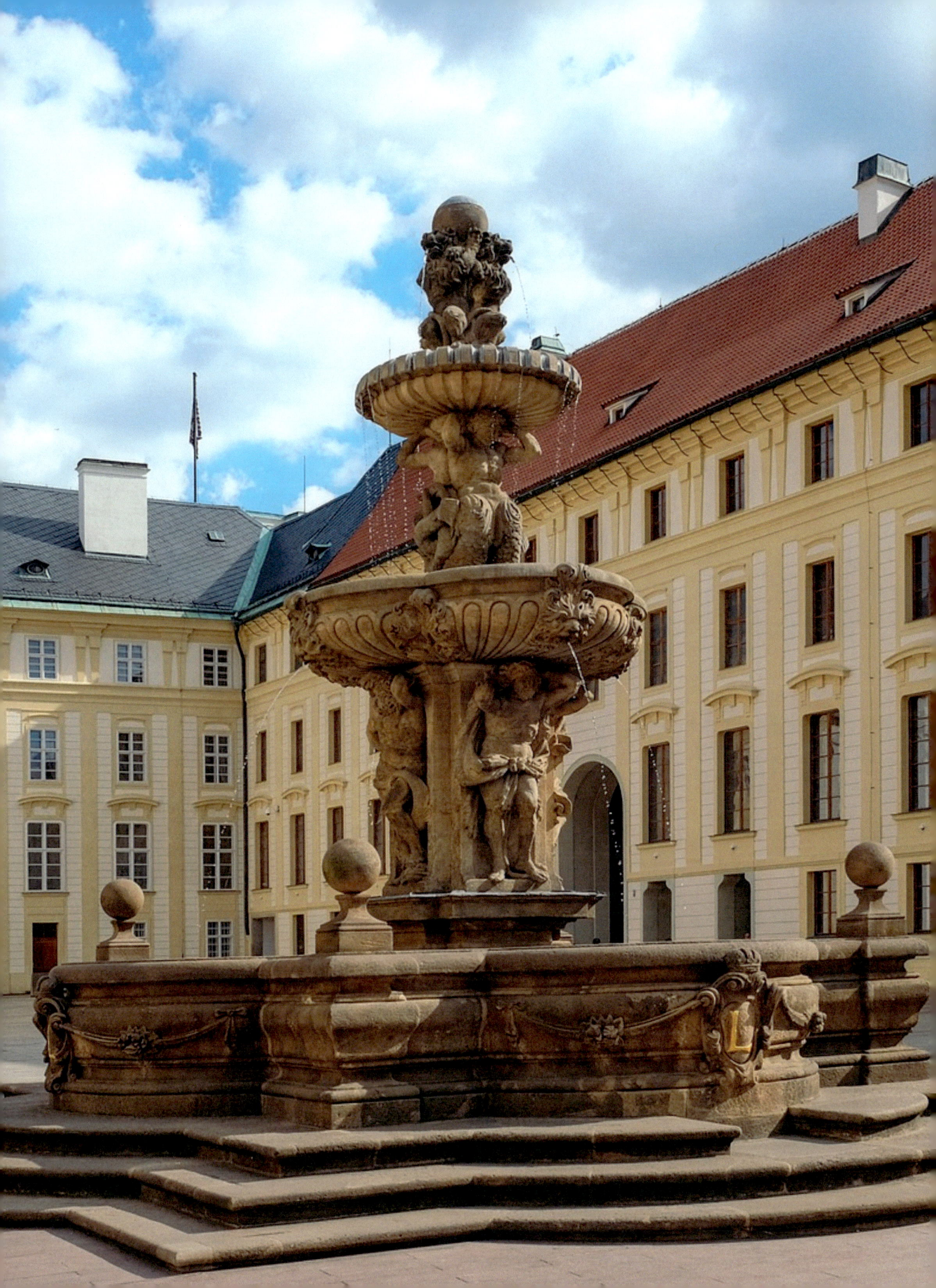

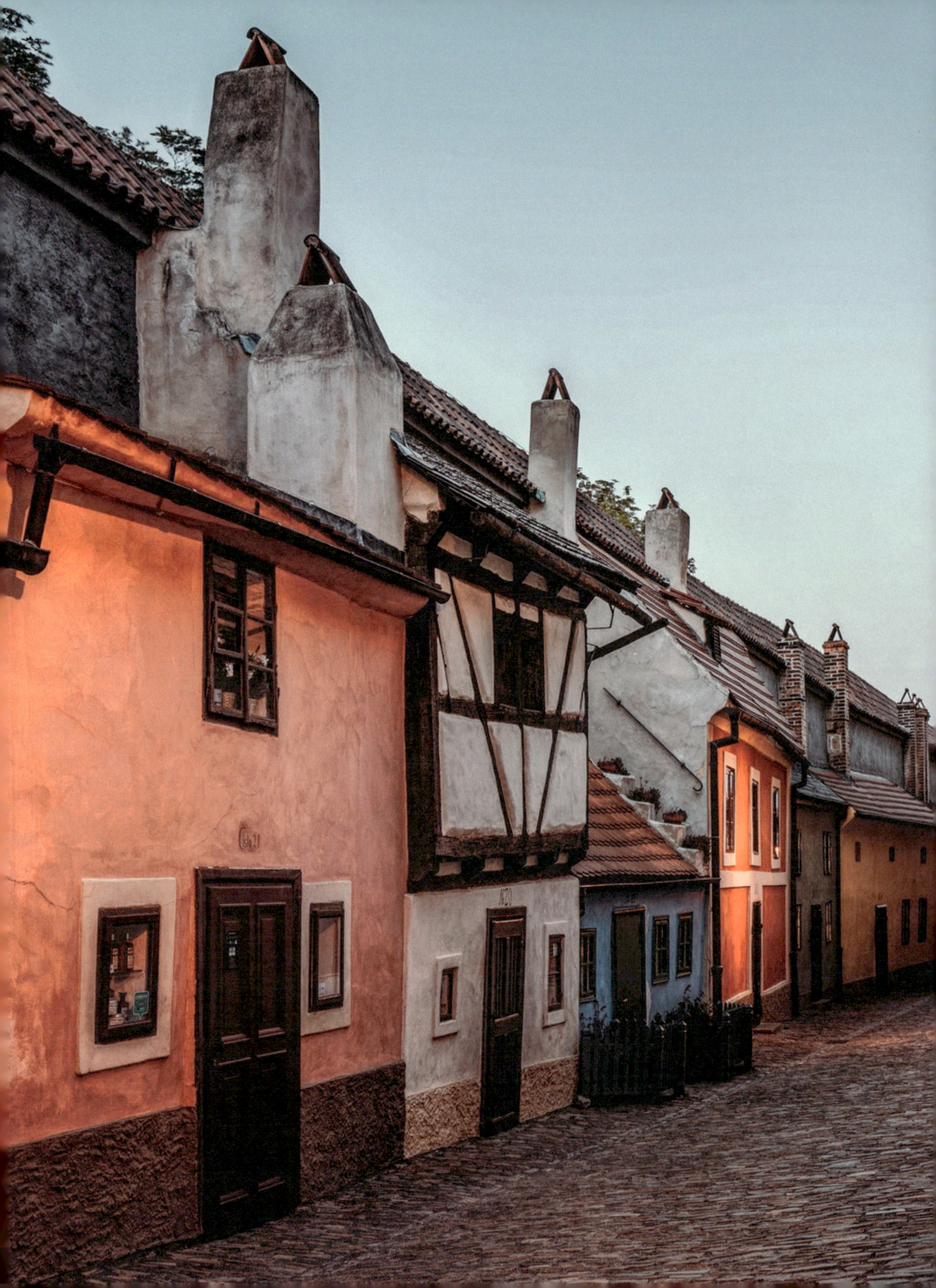

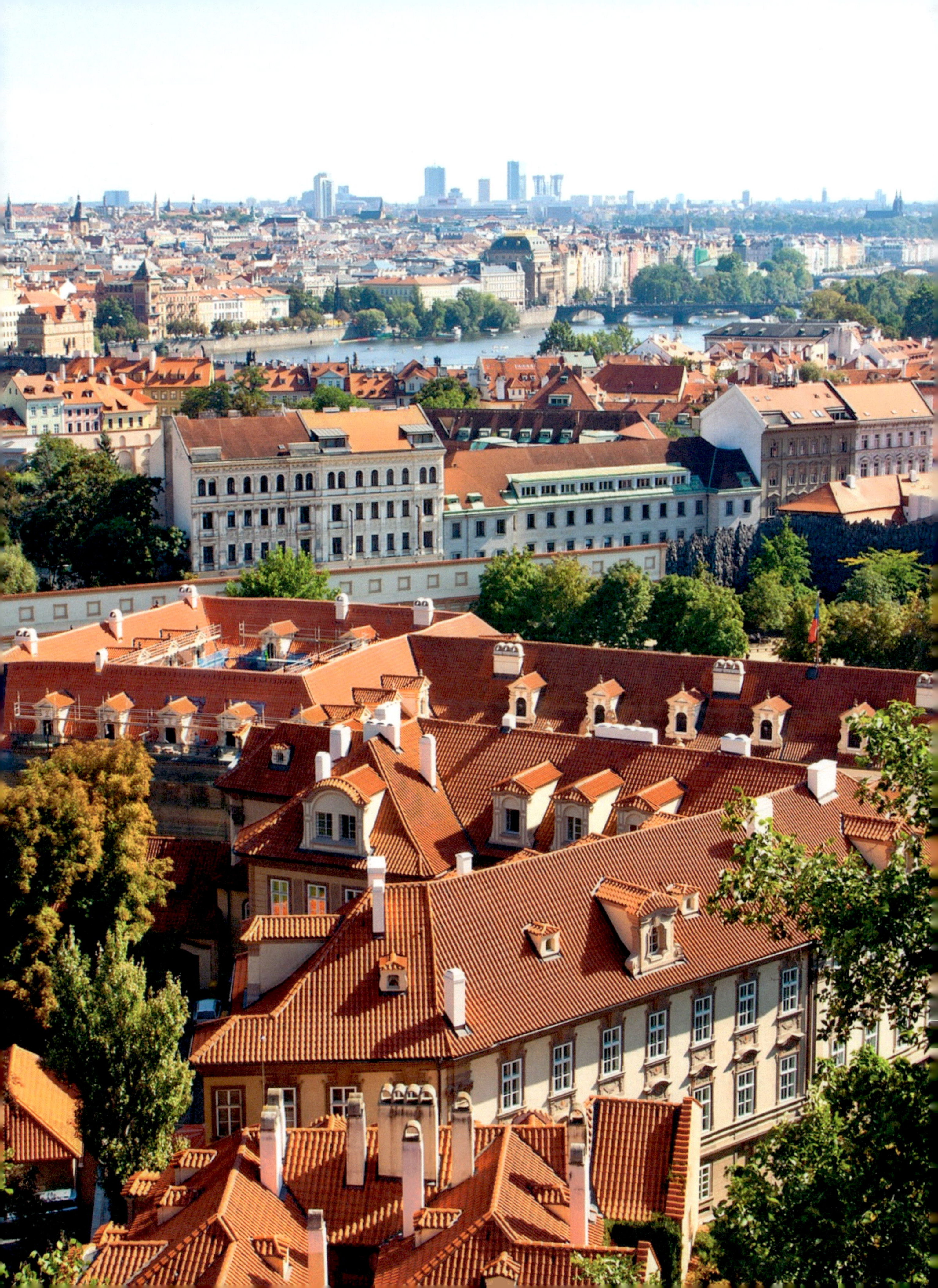

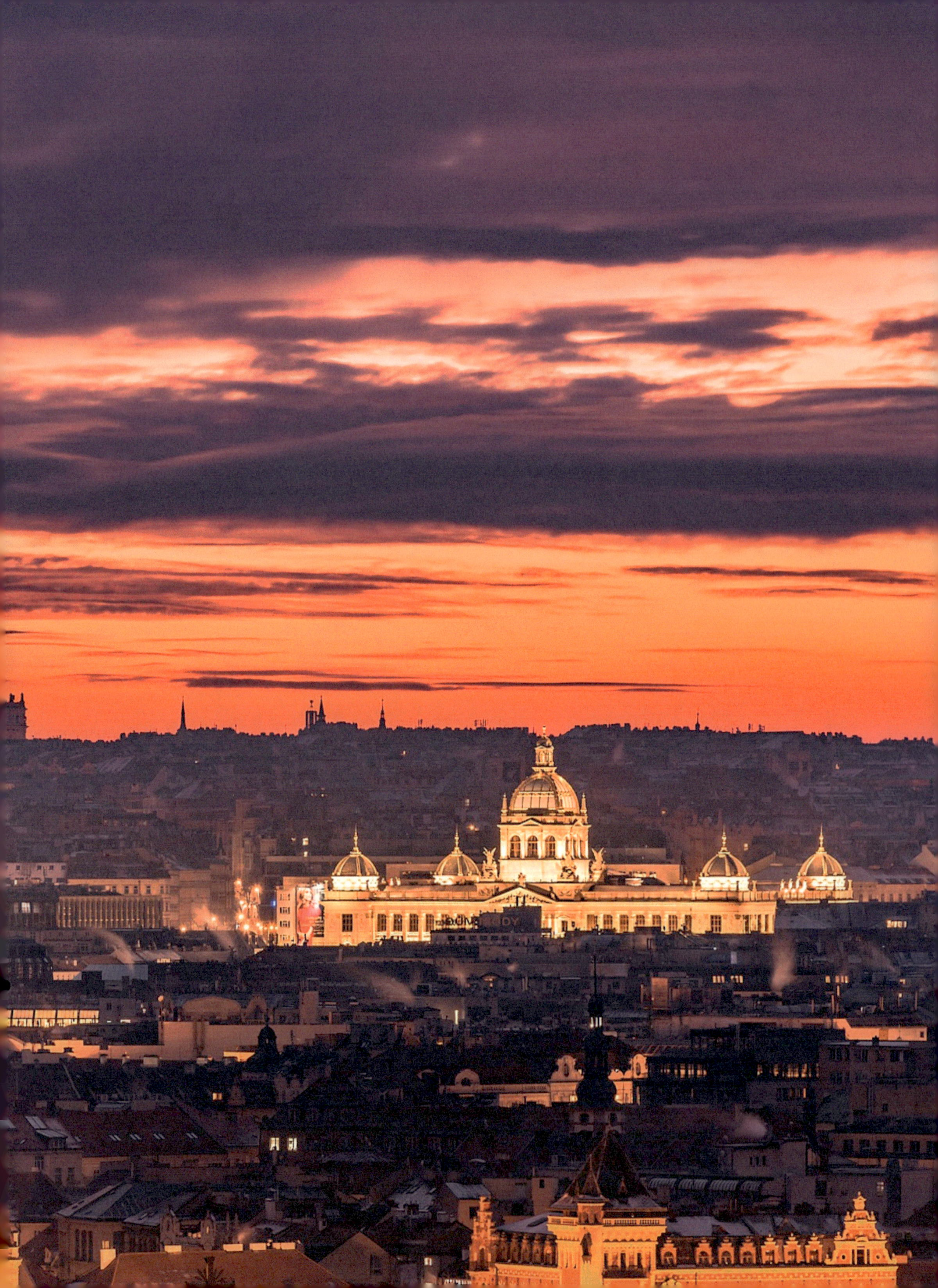

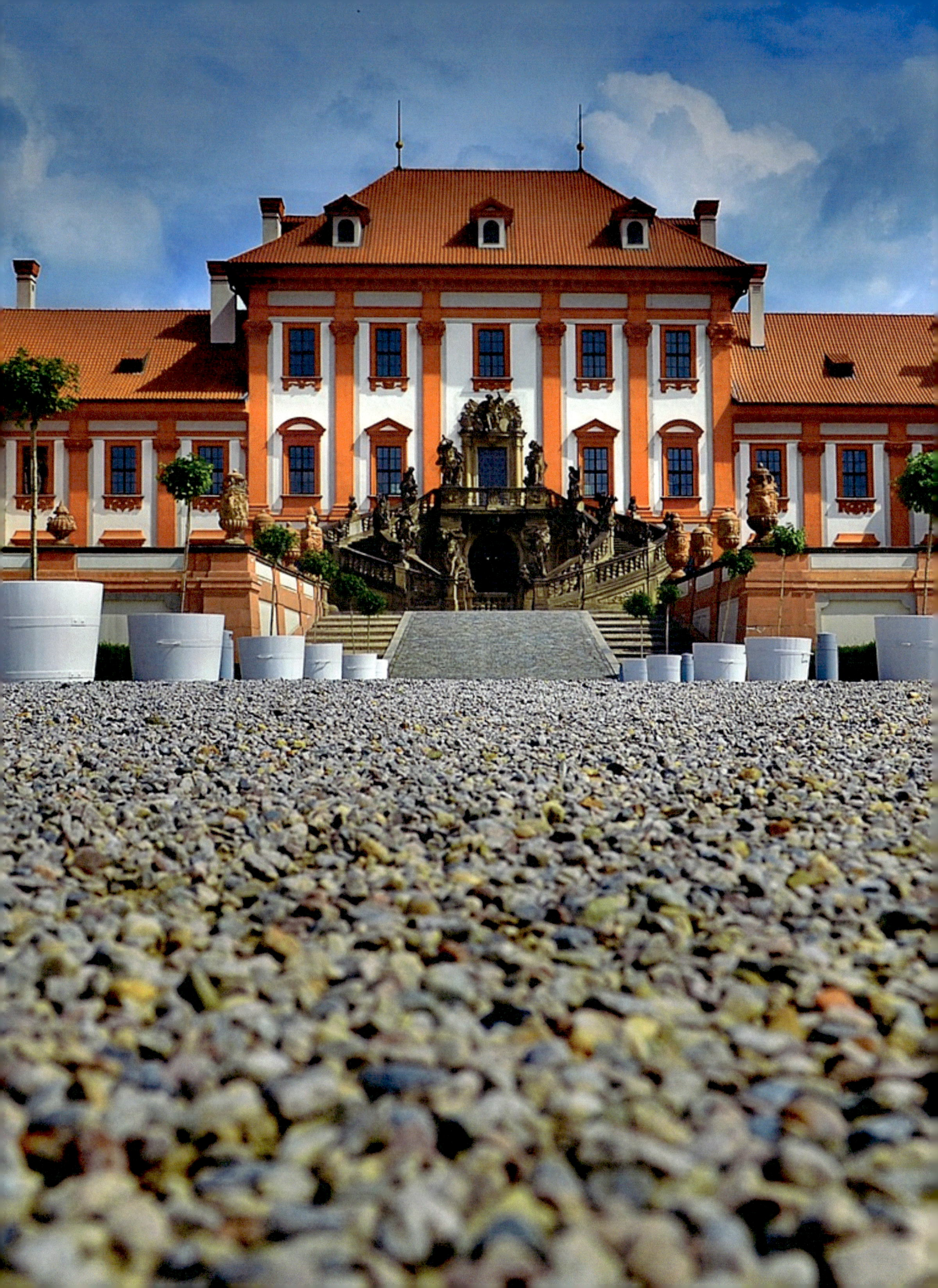

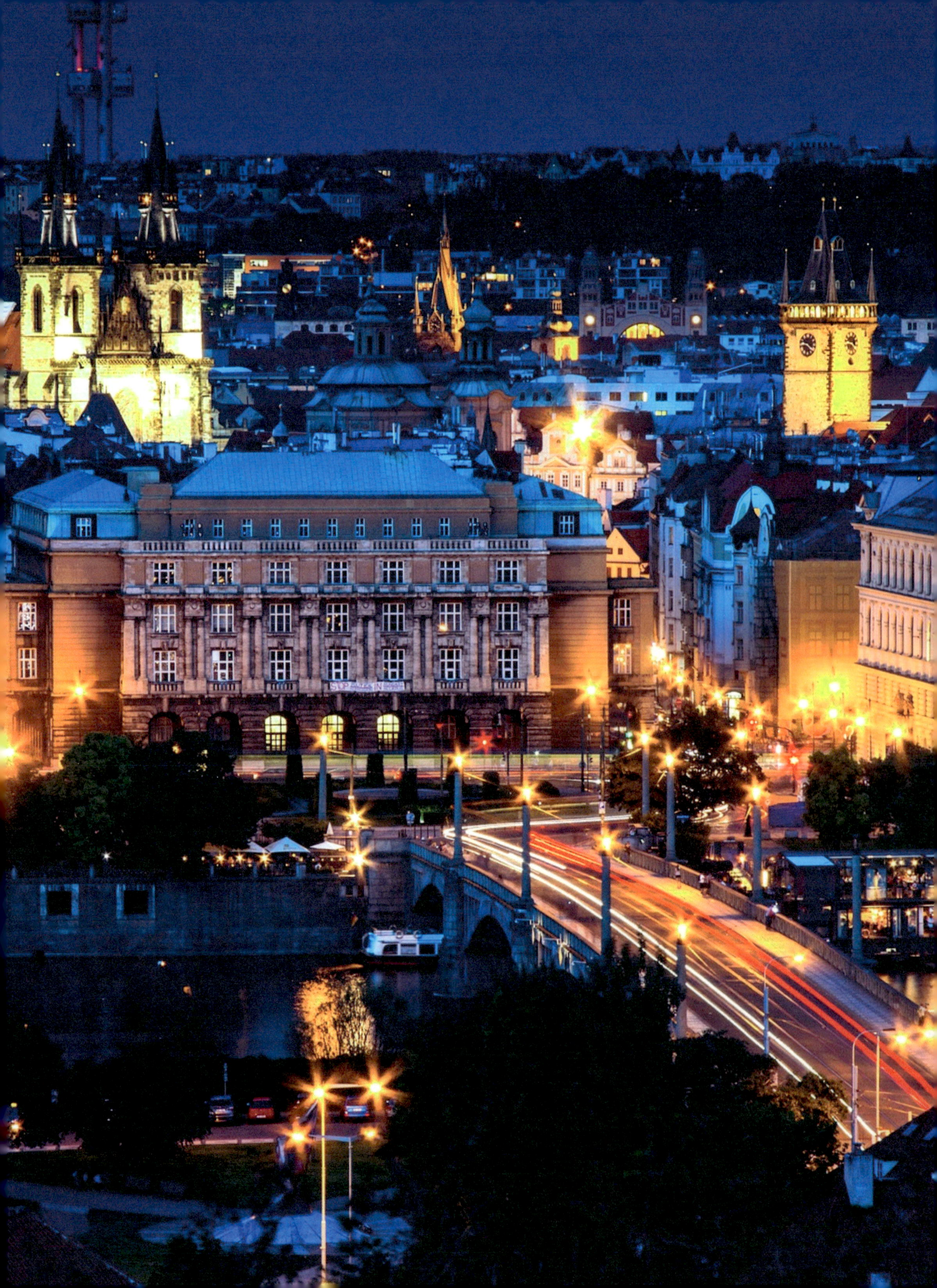

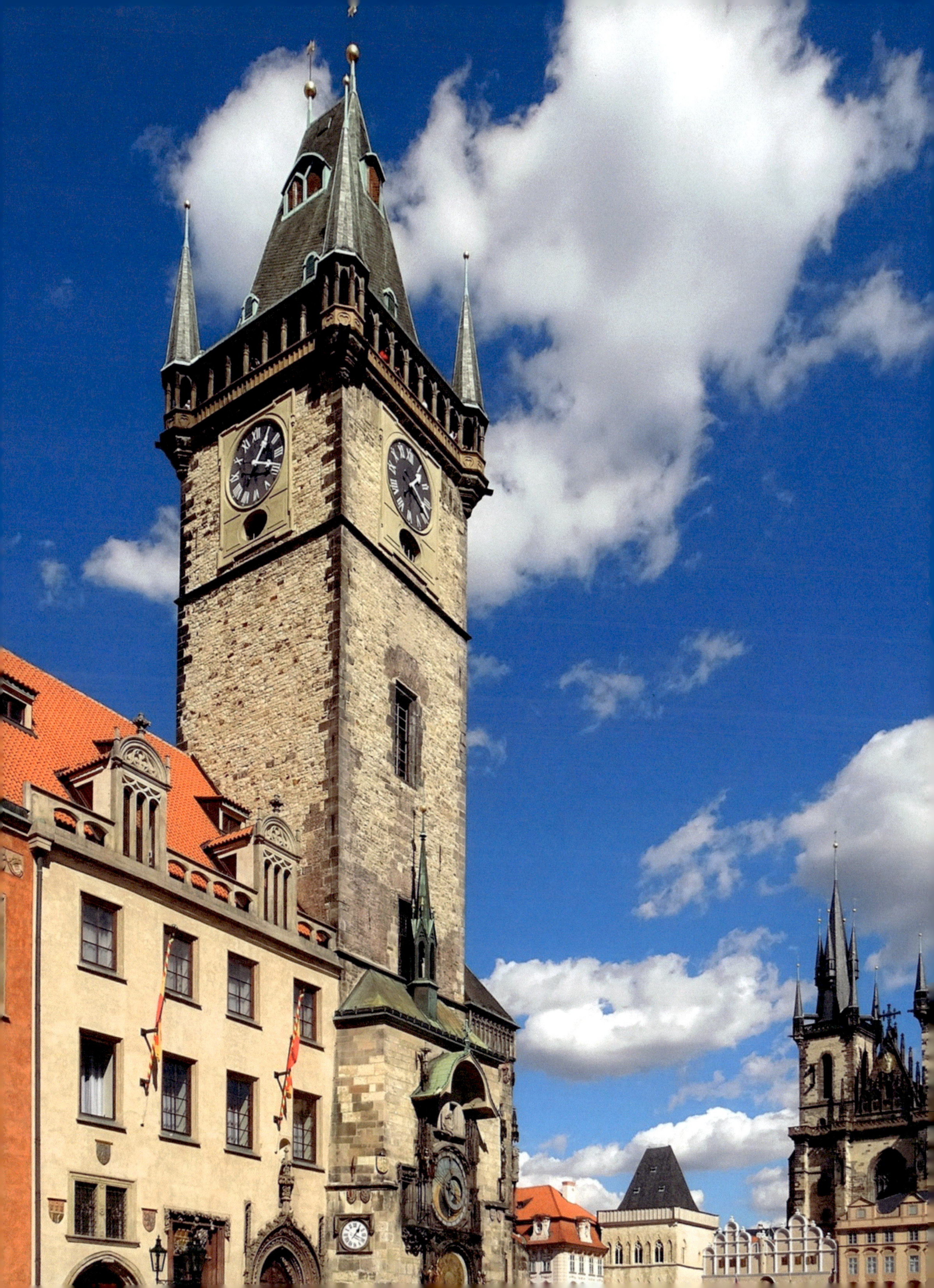

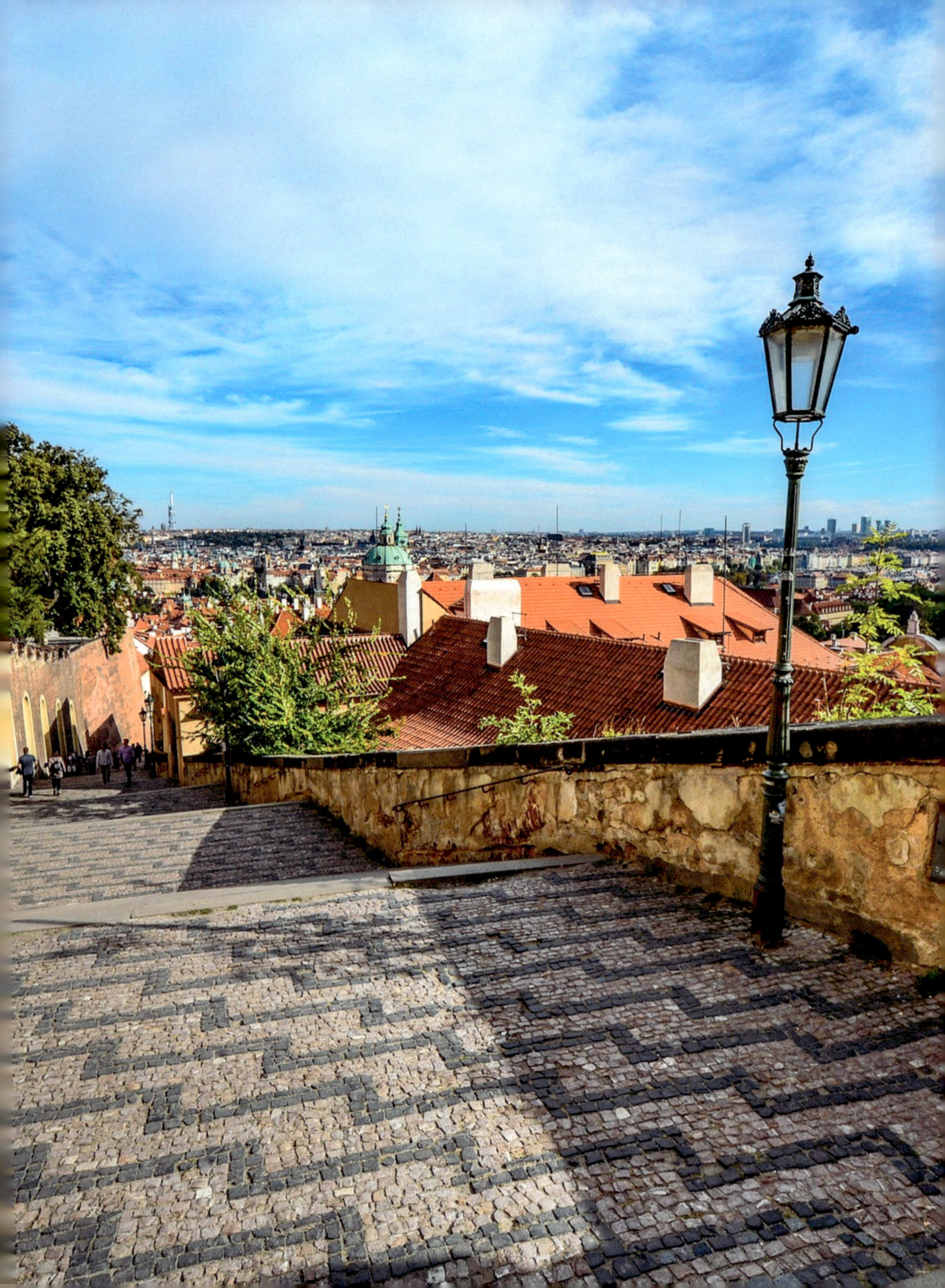

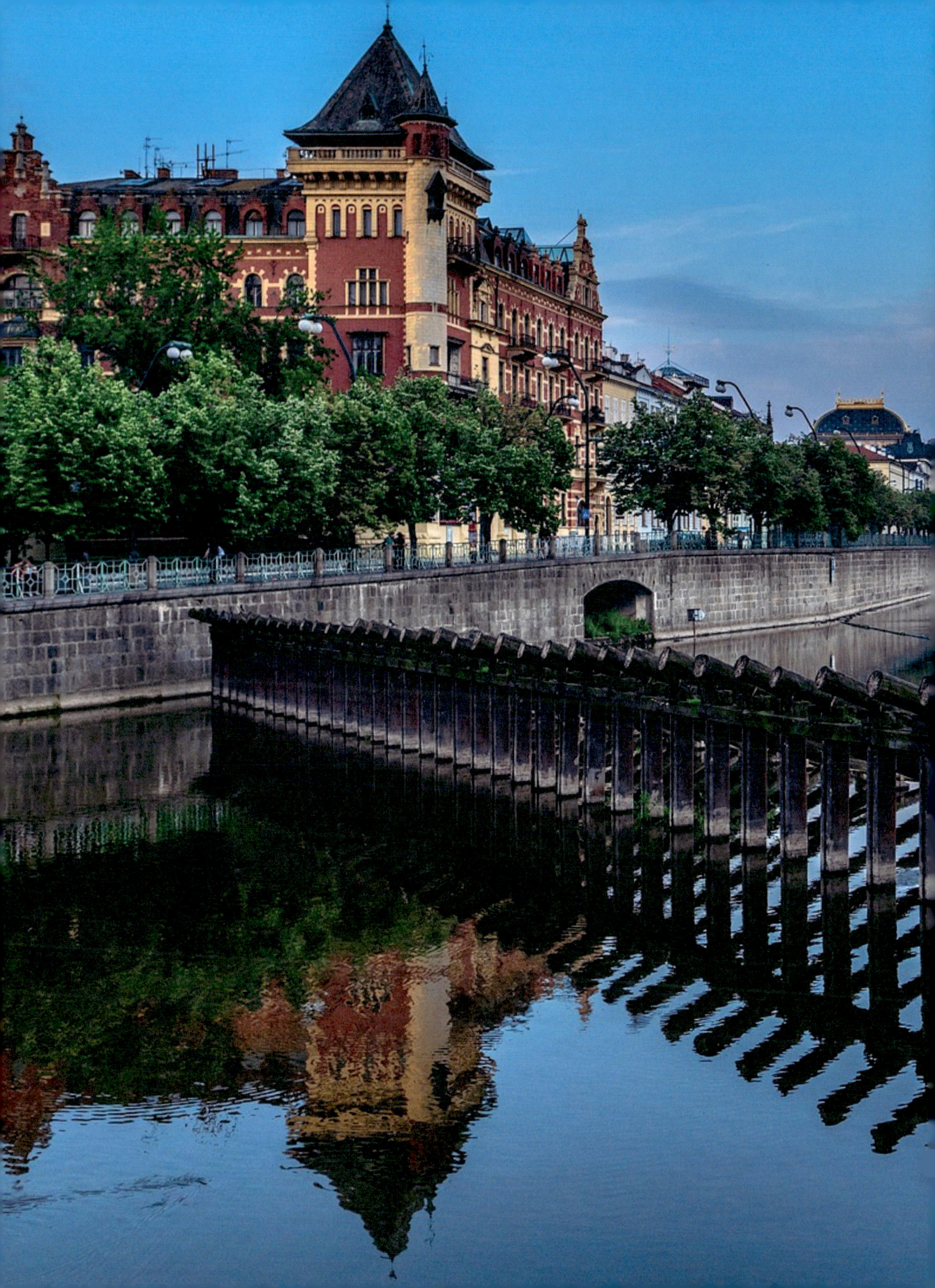

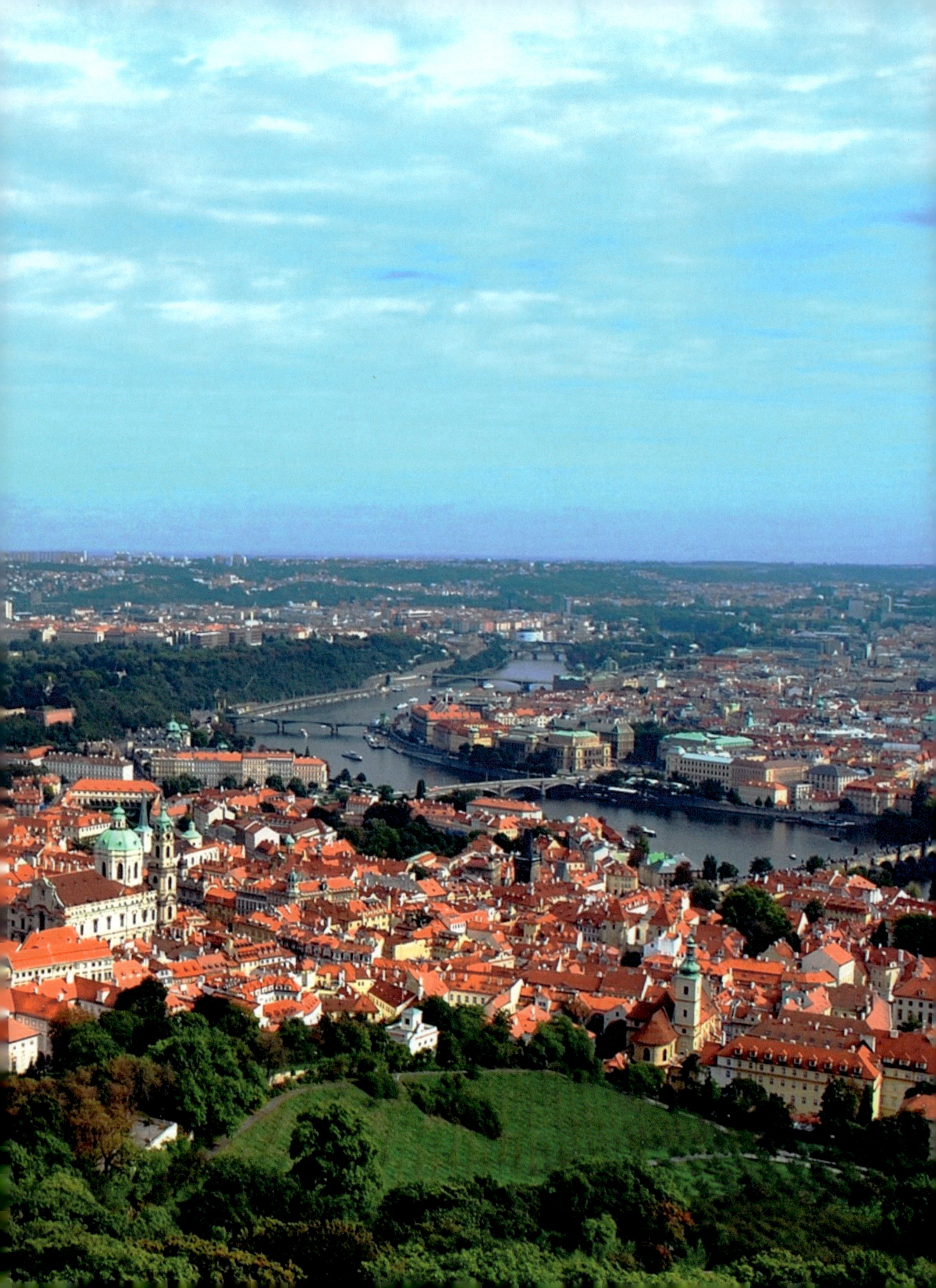

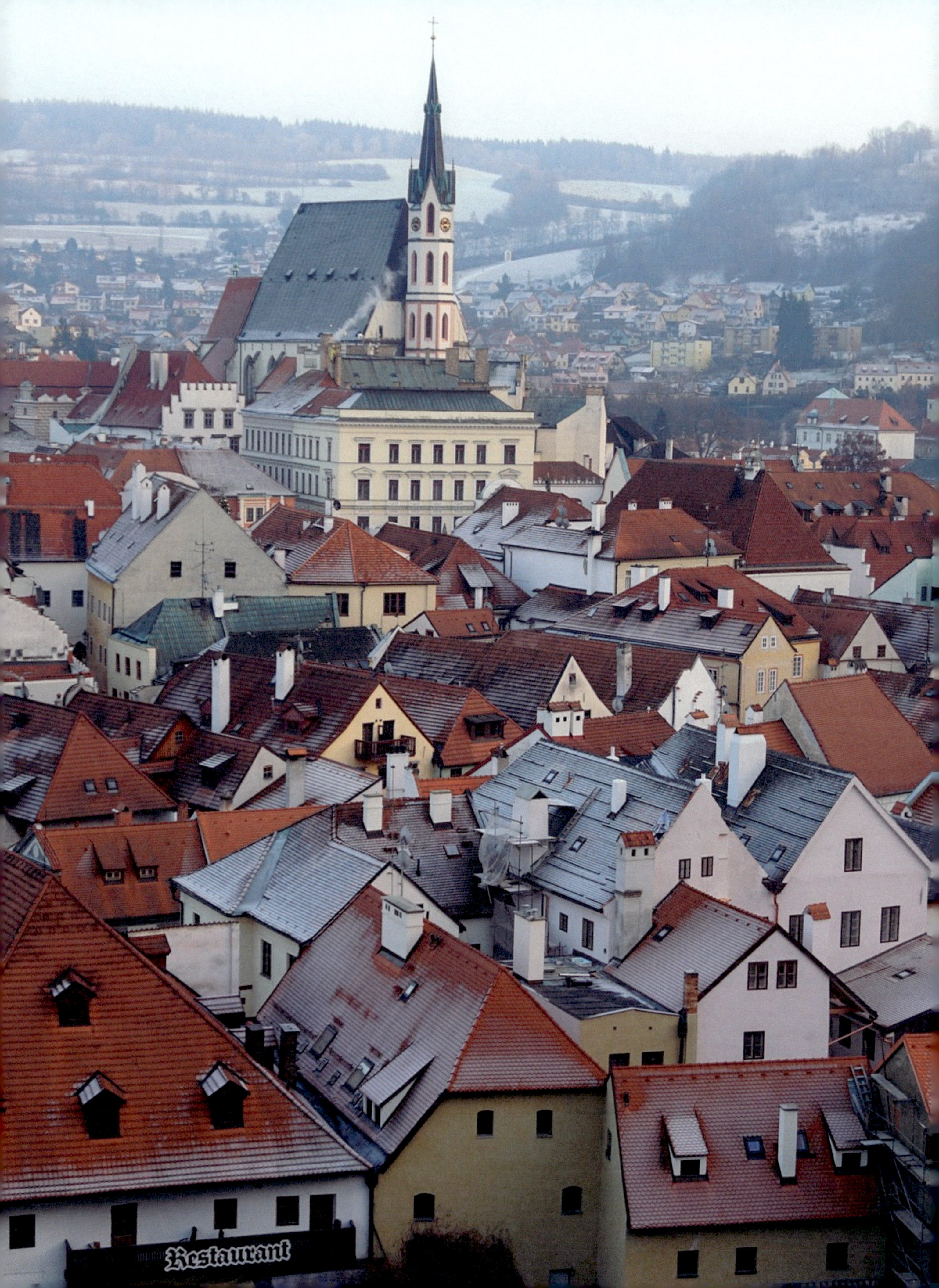
Restaurant

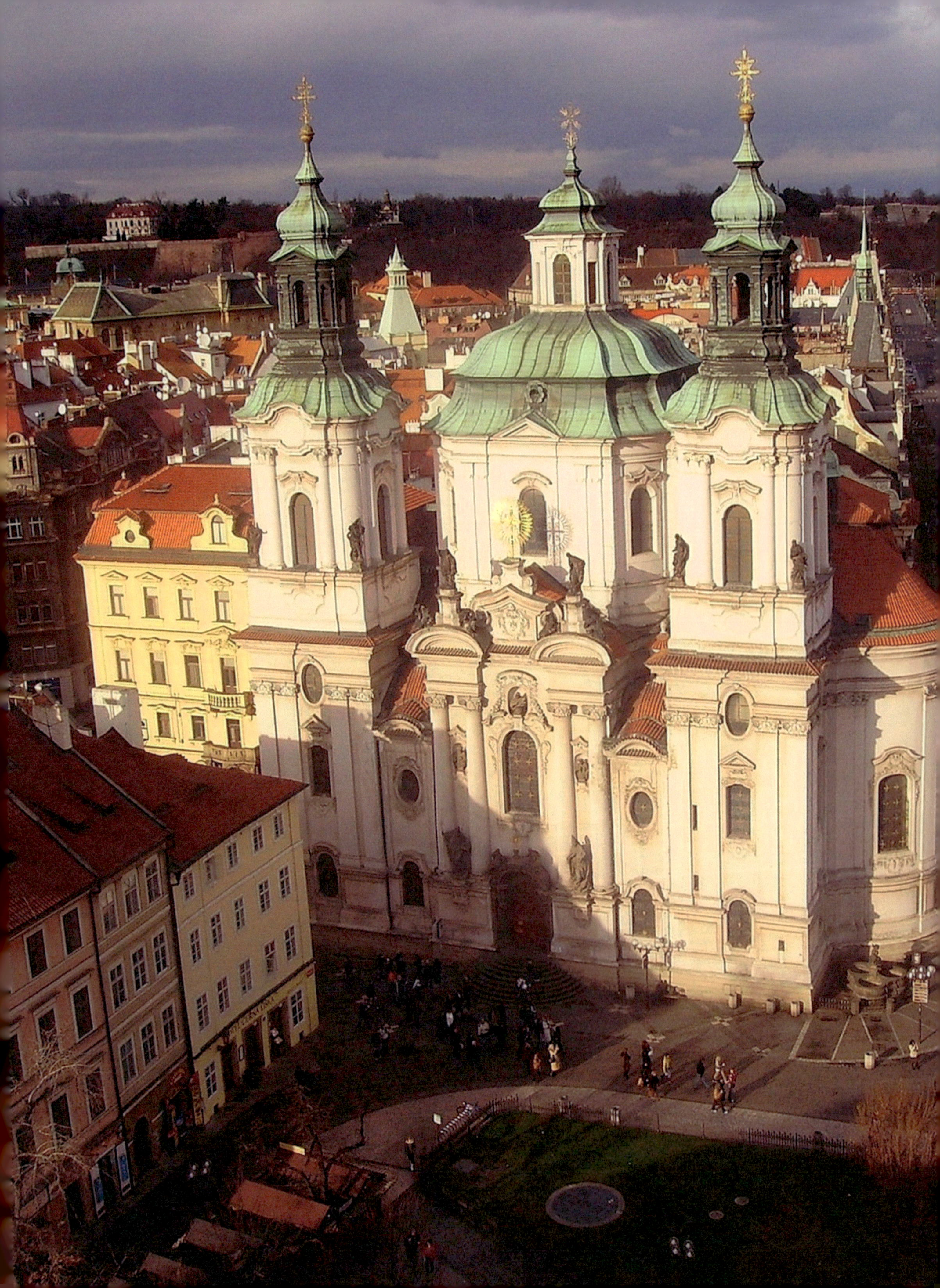

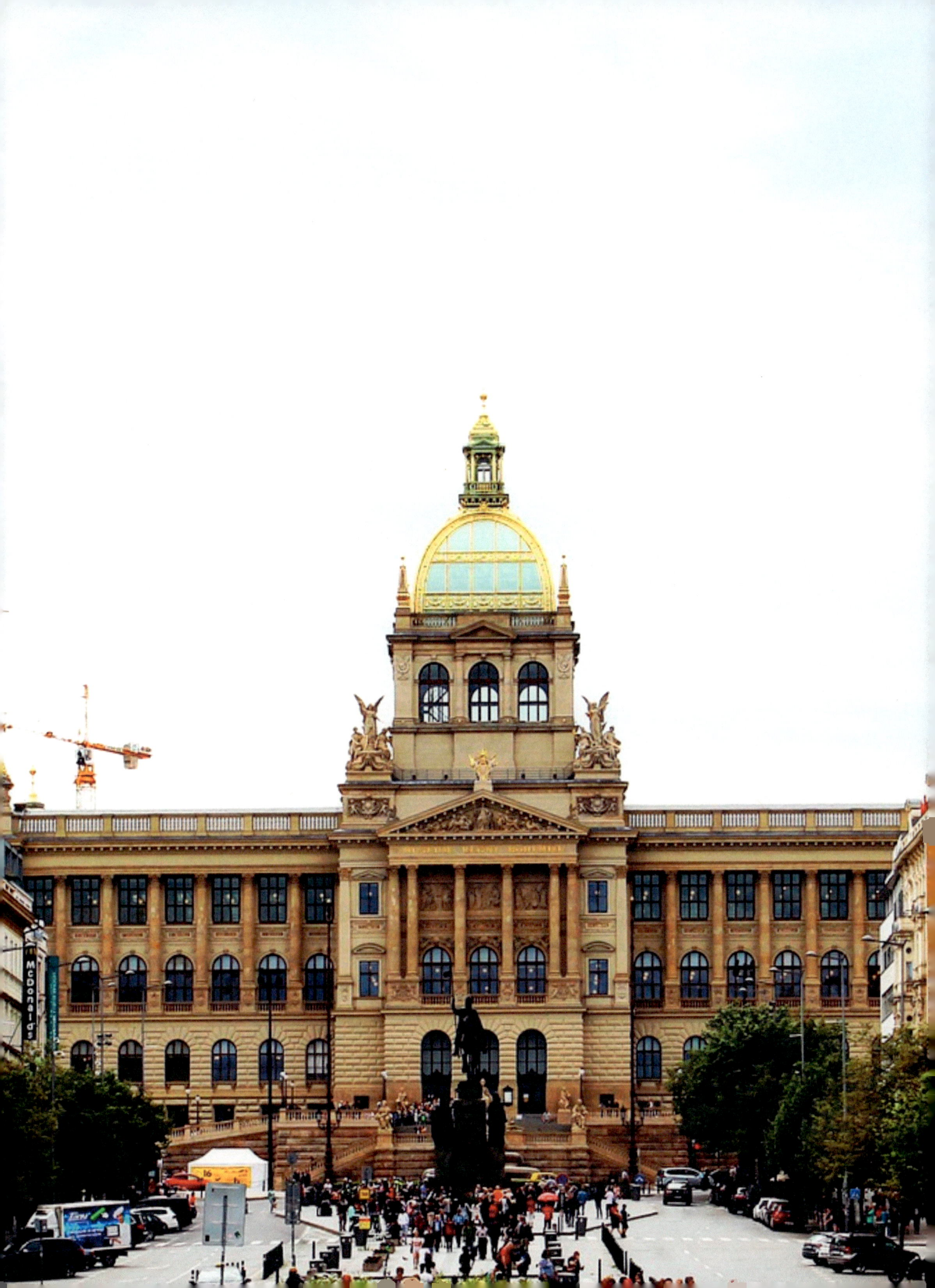
McDonalds

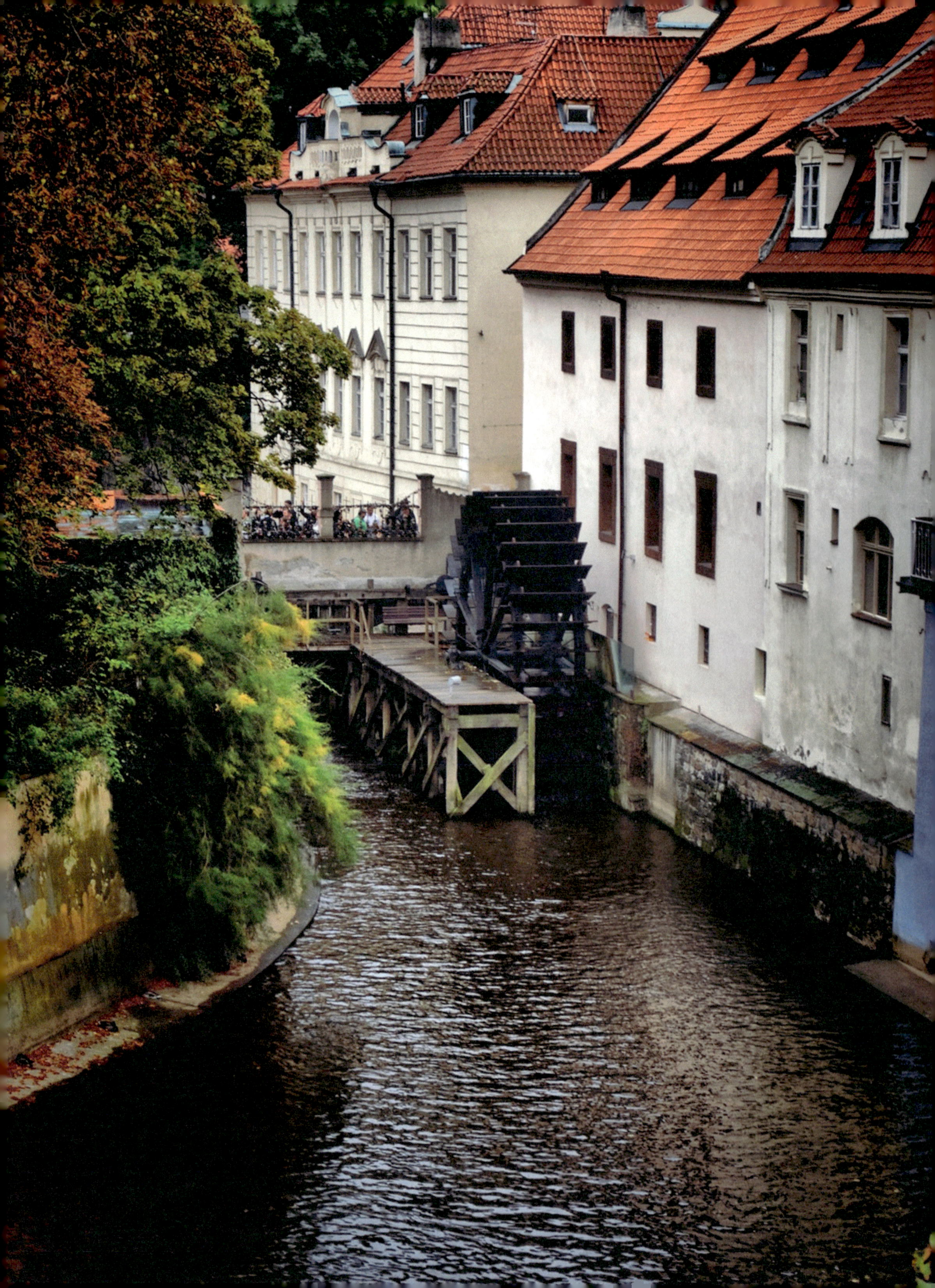

Made in United States
Troutdale, OR
10/15/2023

13720594R00026